T0361257

ROUTLEDGE LIBRARY EDITIONS:
THE AUTOMOBILE INDUSTRY

Volume 7

SHORT-SIGHTED SOLUTIONS: TRADE AND ENERGY POLICIES FOR THE U.S. AUTO INDUSTRY

SHORT-SIGHTED SOLUTIONS: TRADE AND ENERGY POLICIES FOR THE U.S. AUTO INDUSTRY

ROBERT E. SCOTT

Routledge
Taylor & Francis Group

LONDON AND NEW YORK

First published in 1994 by Garland Publishing, Inc.

This edition first published in 2018
by Routledge
2 Park Square, Milton Park, Abingdon, Oxon OX14 4RN

and by Routledge
711 Third Avenue, New York, NY 10017

Routledge is an imprint of the Taylor & Francis Group, an informa business

© 1994 Robert E. Scott

All rights reserved. No part of this book may be reprinted or reproduced or utilised in any form or by any electronic, mechanical, or other means, now known or hereafter invented, including photocopying and recording, or in any information storage or retrieval system, without permission in writing from the publishers.

Trademark notice: Product or corporate names may be trademarks or registered trademarks, and are used only for identification and explanation without intent to infringe.

British Library Cataloguing in Publication Data
A catalogue record for this book is available from the British Library

ISBN: 978-1-138-73855-3 (Set)
ISBN: 978-1-315-16182-2 (Set) (ebk)
ISBN: 978-1-138-06150-7 (Volume 7) (hbk)
ISBN: 978-1-315-16227-0 (Volume 7) (ebk)

Publisher's Note
The publisher has gone to great lengths to ensure the quality of this reprint but points out that some imperfections in the original copies may be apparent.

Disclaimer
The publisher has made every effort to trace copyright holders and would welcome correspondence from those they have been unable to trace.

SHORT-SIGHTED SOLUTIONS

TRADE AND ENERGY POLICIES FOR THE U.S. AUTO INDUSTRY

ROBERT E. SCOTT

GARLAND PUBLISHING, INC.
NEW YORK & LONDON / 1994

Copyright © 1994 Robert E. Scott
All rights reserved

Library of Congress Cataloging-in-Publication Data

cott, Robert E., 1953–
    Short-sighted solutions : trade and energy policies for the U.S.
auto industry / Robert E. Scott.
        p.   cm. — (Foreign economic policy of the United States)
    Includes bibliographical references and index.
    ISBN 0–8153–1600–3 (alk. paper)
    1. Automobile industry and trade—Government policy—United
States.   2. Motor vehicle industry—Government policy—United
States.   3. Export controls—Japan.   4. Automobiles—Fuel
consumption—Law and legislation—United States.   5. Automobiles—
Pollution control devices—Law and legislation—United States.
I. Title.   II. Series.
HD9710.U52S34   1994
338.4'76292'0973—dc20   93–43002
                                                                  CIP

Printed on acid-free, 250-year-life paper
Manufactured in the United States of America

To the memory of
my grandmother,

Lois White Eck

CONTENTS

ILLUSTRATIONS

PREFACE

The U.S. auto industry has undergone continued change since the research for this book was completed in 1989. The U.S. economy experienced a mild recession in 1990 and 1991 which severely depressed auto industry output and profits for several years. The dollar has depreciated steadily versus the Japanese Yen throughout the 1990s, reaching the 100 Yen/Dollar level and trading between 100 and 110 in late 1993. This sustained depreciation has increased the costs of Japanese firms supplying the U.S. vehicle market, reducing their share of the market (including vehicles assembled in U.S. transplant facilities) from 28.2% for the 1992 model year to 27.1% in 1993.[1] However, Japanese auto firms represent a continuing threat to U.S.-based producers and to employment in North American auto production. This preface will briefly review recent developments in the industry and will summarize the findings of several recent studies of the competitive problems of this industry. It will conclude with comments on policy options for the automotive sector.

A. Conditions in the U.S. Vehicle Market: 1980-1993

The research presented here concerns the effects of trade and energy policies on the price and sales (volume) levels of U.S.-based automobile producers between 1981 and 1986. Truck markets are not included in the formal model, but they are covered in the literature review in chapter II. The truck and automotive sectors are closely linked. Trade and energy regulations affect the mix of vehicles produced and sold in the two markets. These regulatory regimes have also had a substantial influence on the competitiveness of the U.S. auto industry, in ways which were not foreseen when the policies were developed in the 1970s and 1980s.

The truck market received a substantial increase in protection in August of 1980 when cab/chassis "kits" which were being imported from Japan, were reclassified as trucks by the U.S. Dept. of Commerce, raising the effective tariff rate on these units from 4% to 25%.[2] U.S. small truck imports have been subject to the 25% tariff since the early 1960s.   The auto market was protected from Japanese imports, beginning in May 1981, by a series of Voluntary Restraint Agreements (VRAs) which limited exports to the U.S.[3] The VRAs were first set at 1.8 million units in 1981. They were expanded to 2.3 million units in April 1985 and maintained at that level through 1992.[4]

The VRAs and the truck tariff both created incentives which encouraged foreign producers to assemble vehicles in the U.S. Transplant production by Asian-based firms, which was nonexistent before 1982, has increased steadily in the past decade and reached 18% of total U.S. and Canadian vehicle production in 1992.[5] Howes (1993) asserts that "transplant production is little better than imports and does not help to revitalize the U.S. automobile industry as a whole". This conclusion is based on the observation that transplants use a high proportion of imported parts and therefore have a low level of domestic labor content. Howes estimates that in the long run "no less than 50 percent (by value) of the parts used to assemble vehicles in transplants will remain imported, including core parts of vehicles such as the drivetrain".

In the 1980s and 1990s, as the value of the Dollar declined, Japanese transplant production capacity in North America increased to over 2 million units per year (2.1 million transplant cars were produced in the 1993 model year, 99% in Japanese owned or operated facilities). An additional 1.2 million units of transplant capacity were planned in 1993 (Howes, 1993).

Import Penetration
U.S.-based producers were much more competitive in the truck than in the auto market segments, in part because of differences in the trade policies applied to these products. The market share of imported trucks in the U.S. increased from 7.2 percent in 1976 to 19.5 percent in 1980, as shown in Figure 1. Imports never captured more than 20% of the truck market. The truck segment import share peaked in 1986 and has declined steadily since then. This pattern is closely correlated with the trade-weighted value of the Dollar, which was highly overvalued in the early 1980s, reaching a peak real value in 1985 which was 59% higher than its level in 1979, and declined in value between 1985 and 1992.[6]

The import share of the auto market peaked in 1987, one year later than in trucks, reached a maximum of 31.2 percent, and failed to decline as rapidly as truck imports, as shown in Figure 1. These data suggest that U.S.-based firms were much less competitive in the auto than in the truck market.

Figure 1

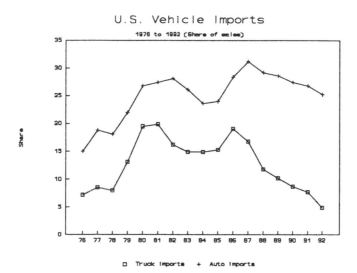

Source: *Citibase.*

The disparities in U.S. competitiveness in the truck and auto segments are highlighted much more sharply in Figure 2, which plots the combined market share of imports and transplants. Transplant production accelerated in the late 1980s, as U.S. vehicle imports began to decline. Autos accounted for 90% of transplant output in 1992. Foreign-based producers captured over half of the total U.S. auto market in 1991 and 1992, and about 13% of the truck market. Furthermore, the truck share of imports and transplants was declining between 1986 and 1992, while the auto share was growing rapidly. These data suggest that the competitive problems of U.S. motor vehicle producers are concentrated in the auto segment. The rapid growth of truck demand in the 1970s and 1980s has partially offset the decline of U.S.-based auto production and of North American vehicle output and employment.

Figure 2

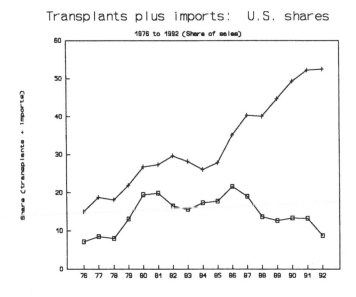

Source: *Citibase; Automotive News*, January 11, 1993, p. 51, and
Ward's Automotive Yearbook, 1992, p. 159.

Fuel Economy Regulations

The U.S. auto and truck markets have also been affected by the
development of fuel economy regulations in the 1970s and 1980s. The
Corporate Auto Fuel Economy (CAFE) standards and the Gas Guzzler
tax both discouraged manufacturers from building and selling large cars
in the U.S. during the 1980s, as shown in chapters V and VI. What is
less well appreciated is that the fuel economy standards have also
created incentives for U.S. vehicle manufacturers to increase the sales
of trucks, compared to autos.

The CAFE standards are applied separately to the truck and auto
fleets sold by each firm in the U.S.[7] In 1991 the auto standard was
27.5 miles per gallon, and firms exceeding this standard were assessed

fines. The 1991 CAFE standard for trucks was 20.5 miles per gallon. Thus a minivan, which could get 23 miles per gallon and was classified as a truck, generated a CAFE credit.[8] However, if the same vehicle were classified as a car it would generate a CAFE penalty. Thus the CAFE rules created incentives for U.S. firms to produce more small trucks and fewer large automobiles such as station wagons.

The truck segment of U.S. vehicle sales increased dramatically in the 1980s and 1990s. In 1980 20.4% of all vehicles sold in the U.S. were trucks. In the 1993 model year over 5 million trucks were sold in the U.S., 38.2% of total vehicle sales.[9] Fuel economy regulations, lower gas prices and the truck tariff all contributed to the growth of the truck segment. This growth also reflects change in corporate strategy and shifts in consumer preferences during this period. Growth in the truck segment is responsible for most of the output gains experienced by U.S. producers in the early 1990s. U.S. vehicle exports outside of North America also began to increase in the early 1990s, and trucks (including minivans) are a major component of that export growth.[10] The competitiveness of U.S. truck producers can be traced, in part, to the expansion of the truck tariff and the constraints imposed by U.S. fuel economy regulations as these began to affect producers in the mid-1980s.

I examined a series of hypotheses concerning the effects of fuel economy regulations on the price and sales levels of U.S.-based auto producers in an extension of the research reported here (Scott, 1993). I estimated that fuel economy regulations reduced sales by 1.7% between 1984 and 1986 and increased average prices by 1.4%, with all of the effects concentrated in the large car segments of the U.S. auto market.

Pricing Patterns

Auto prices were influenced by a number of factors in the 1970s and 1980s, including increasingly stringent emissions controls, safety regulations, and trade protection. One of the principle goals of this study is to identify and estimate the effects of the VRAs on domestic auto prices, by firm and size class. The price effects of the VRAs significantly influenced the competitiveness of U.S.- and foreign-based producers. These effects are considered in the context of the policy discussion below. Figure 3 summarizes the overall price trends in the auto market, for foreign and domestic producers, between 1977 and the first five months of 1993.

Prior to the 1980s, imported vehicles competed in the U.S. market on the basis of low prices, with the exception of European luxury sedans. However, Japanese producers caught and surpassed U.S. firms in quality and price levels in the early 1980s. The increase in import prices between 1980 and 1985 is particularly remarkable. During this period, the dollar was gaining value rapidly, as noted above, which reduced the cost of all imported goods. However, the average imported car increased in value by $2,736 (in real 1983 dollars) between 1980 and 1985, an increase of 29.6%. Most of this increase was associated with the costs of protection (the effects of the VRAs on the transaction prices of imports are not calculated in this study, which considers only the wholesale prices of imports).[11]

Figure 3

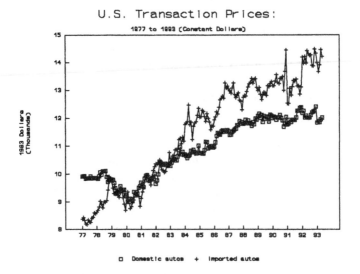

Sources: *Citibase.*

After 1985 the average price of imported vehicles exceeds domestic prices by substantial margins. Higher import prices reflect both quota premiums and the quality upgrading effects of the VRAs, which have been noted by Feenstra (1985b) and are discussed in the text.

Competitive Dynamics

The 1980s and early 1990s have been difficult for U.S.-based auto producers and disastrous for many workers in this industry. Total U.S. vehicle sales reach peak levels in excess of 15 million units per year in the mid-1980s and then collapsed to 12.3 million units in 1990. Total sales were only 13.6 million units in the 1993 model year because of the slow rate of recovery of the domestic economy. The share of the domestic vehicle market (trucks plus autos) captured by imports plus transplants increased from 19.7% in 1979 to 34.1% in 1992, and the market share of the big-3 U.S. producers declined accordingly.

Employment in the U.S. motor vehicle industry has declined for four reasons during this period: 1) increased import market share; 2) the rise in transplant production; 3) rapid productivity growth; and 4) the slow recovery from the recession of 1990-91. Peak U.S. employment levels in motor vehicle production occurred in 1979 (1.05 million workers) and 1985 (0.883 million).[12] By 1992, 74,000 jobs had been lost, relative to employment in 1985.

The United Auto Workers (UAW) union has been especially hard hit by the growth of the transplant firms which, with only one exception, are non-union plants. The UAW has lost representation elections in several new transplant facilities. Thus UAW membership employed in auto assembly and parts production has declined more rapidly than total employment in this industry.

Most of the decline in the market share of U.S.-based producers has been absorbed by General Motors (GM), which saw its share of the auto market fall from 45.9% in 1980 to 34.0% in the 1993 model year. The later figure includes captive imports and transplant production. GM transplant and captive import sales were 3.2% of U.S. auto sales in 1991, the most recent period for which such data is available. Therefore domestic cars made by GM held a 1993 market share of approximately 31% of U.S. auto sales, for a combined decline in domestic production of 15% of the U.S. auto market, relative to its share in 1980.

Ford's share of the total U.S. vehicle market increased from 24.4% to 25.4% between 1992 and 1993, and Chrysler's share grew from 12.9% to 14.1%, while GM's share of total vehicle sales fell from 34.6% to 33.4%. 1993 shares reflect long-term gains since 1980 of 2.9% of the U.S. market for Ford and 4.6% for Chrysler. The current market shares of these producers do include transplant and captive imports and thus overstate their competitiveness. However, the most fundamental challenge facing the U.S. motor vehicle industry remains the question of what should be done about the continuing collapse of GM. In 1980 Chrysler was bailed out by the U.S. government because of the potentially disruptive effects its collapse would have on the domestic economy. In 1980 Chrysler had a 9.5% share of the U.S. vehicle market. GM has yielded 15% of the U.S. market to imports and transplant products since 1980, or about one and one half times the output of Chrysler in 1980.

Cost and Productivity Differences

High manufacturing costs are one of the fundamental causes of the competitive problems of U.S.-based firms. This issue is analyzed in chapter II, pp. 18-23, below. The literature on the Manufacturing Cost Differential (MCD) through the mid-1980s is reviewed there. This material is relevant to the current discussion but must be updated. In particular, most of the analysis in Chapter II assumes Yen/Dollar exchange rates in the range of 210-215, versus levels of 100-110 Yen per Dollar which prevailed in late 1993.

Despite the recent U.S. devaluation, domestic producers still confront cost problems. Prestowitz and Willen (1992) of the Economic Strategy Institute (ESI) claim that at full capacity (and excluding the costs of retiree benefits), Ford and Chrysler's costs are below the Japanese average by $990 and $519 per car, respectively. At full capacity, GM's costs still exceeded the Japanese average by $1,048 per car. However, at actual 1992 operating levels U.S. firms had much lower levels of capacity utilization and much higher retiree and health costs than their Japanese counterparts. Including these cost "penalties" results in a cost disadvantage of $568 per car for Ford, $1,184 for Chrysler and $3,363 for GM. Prestowitz and Willen claim that the Japanese market is closed to U.S. exports, giving Japanese producers an unfair advantage because of their higher rates of capacity utilization.[13]

Womack, Jones and Roos (1991) of the MIT International Motor Vehicle Program (IMVP) claim that Japanese producers, and Toyota in particular, have developed an entirely new mode of "lean production" which uses "half the human effort in the factory, half the manufacturing space, half the investment in tools, half the engineering hours to develop a new product in half the time (Womack, *et al.*, 1991, p. 13)." They claim that lean production is a new development in manufacturing technology which will displace mass production techniques in a wide range of industries in the same way that craft production was displaced in the early part of the twentieth century in the U.S.

Womack, *et al.* claim that Ford and Chrysler have begun to adopt lean production techniques, but that GM has not.[14] They also argue that high levels of *variation* in capacity utilization are inconsistent with lean production techniques. U.S. firms thus suffer from a structural disadvantage compared to their Japanese counterparts because the U.S. economy is characterized by higher levels of cyclical variation in output and demand. Thus Womack, *et al.* place more emphasis on the continuous evolution of production technology than on the static costs of low capacity utilization emphasized by the ESI.

B. Policy Options for the 1990s

The IMVP report states that the problems of the motor vehicle industry are caused by "the resistance of the massive mass-production corporations" including GM to adopting the principles of lean production. Womack, *et al.* suggest that "every mass producer needs a lean competitor located right across the road." They also recommend improvements in financial systems to increase the access of auto producers to sources of new capital. Finally, they recognize that employment losses are likely in the auto sector and suggest that publicly supported job banks and worker retraining programs may be necessary to facilitate adjustment. The IMVP report emphasizes the need for workers to develop new types of skills and for firms to develop new forms of industrial/professional relations and develop career paths which emphasize teamwork, group processes and cooperative workstyles.

Womack, *et al.* do not recommend any form of import or transplant investment restrictions and state that "transplants will keep on growing until the American companies improve their performance and regain the initiative, or are eliminated." They claim that these policies and "full implementation of lean production can eliminate the massive trade deficit in motor vehicles."[15] It is not clear whether this prediction includes motor vehicle parts or just finished vehicles.

Prestowitz and Willen (1992) also suggest that the U.S. industrial financing system needs improvement, and estimate that in the 1980s the cost of capital in the U.S. exceeded that in Japan by 4.9 percentage points. They claim that the U.S. auto industry must become an export sector in order to survive, and argue that opening of the Japanese market to U.S. vehicles is needed to achieve this goal and to eliminate the disparity in capacity utilization which characterizes the U.S. and Japanese industries. They also suggest that health care costs should be socialized to improve the competitiveness of U.S. workers.

Howes (1993) is more concerned than the ESI or IMVP authors with the employment and income effects of allowing transplant producers to capture increasing shares of the U.S. vehicle market. She recommends that the total Japanese market share (imports plus transplants) be limited to 1992 levels (3.9 million vehicles) for five to ten years. She supports measures to improve industry financing and reduce health care costs and also suggests that measures are needed to limit state and local "bidding wars" for plant location.

This study places more emphasis on strategic interactions among market participants than the previously cited reports. The results presented in this book are subjected to a series of more extensive hypothesis tests in a forthcoming paper (Scott, 1993). Using a simplified version of the model developed here, I conclude that the VRAs, in particular, increased the output of small cars made by U.S.-based firms by 13% between 1981 and 1986. They also caused the prices of small cars to increase by 11% and intermediate prices to increase by 3% (with no effect on intermediate output). If U.S.-based producers had exercised greater price restraint during the period of the VRAs--by adopting lean production techniques, reducing short-term profits, or both--then they could have captured much larger shares of both markets during the period in which the VRAs most limited import competition. The import share of the auto market did decline between 1982 and 1985, as shown in Figures 1 and 2, above, but the effects were only temporary.

I conclude, in both this book and in my more recent research, that some form of *quid pro quo* commitment should have been obtained from auto producers in exchange for trade protection. Howes also supports measures which establish "minimum performance requirements" in the areas of productivity, prices and compensation. Several pieces of legislation were submitted to Congress in 1992 which would restrict auto imports (Scott, 1993). The proposed bills all included measures which would encourage U.S.-based auto producers to improve their quality and productivity levels. Thus *quid pro quo* measures are gaining support. Such measures are the first steps in the development of an explicit industrial policy for the auto industry. The fundamental question which must be addressed is whether market forces will be the principle determinants of the adjustment path, or whether some form of market intervention, including both trade restrictions and industrial policy measures, will be employed to guide the development of the domestic motor vehicle industry.

The North American automobile industry has been significantly altered in the past decade by the development of transplant production, which will exceed 25% of assembly capacity within a few years, and by the concomitant elimination of excess capacity by U.S.-based firms. Assembly plants are highly visible and important landmarks in this industry. However, a modern "lean" assembly plant only employs about 2,500 workers. Between 50,000 and 75,000 workers are employed in providing parts and materials for each such facility. The location of parts production plants, with their attendant employment and output, will be the most important battleground of the 1990s.

Whether or not the proposed North American Free Trade Agreement is approved in late 1993, the remainder of the decade will be a period of rapid change in the structure and location of vehicle assembly and parts production. I believe that local content restrictions should be adopted by the U.S. in the 1990s, in combination with a set of industrial policy measures designed to improve the competitiveness of U.S. vehicle producers. Local content measures would require foreign-based producers to assemble a minimum share of vehicles in this market.[16] Howes (1993) also endorses local content proposals.

Despite the steady devaluation of the Dollar, the U.S. experienced a deficit of \$28.9 billion in motor vehicles and parts trade with Japan in 1992, 57.6% of its total trade deficit with Japan.[17] It is unlikely that vehicle export growth will significantly reduce or eliminate this deficit in the 1990s. Thus, if trade balance is to be achieved in this sector, imports will have to be reduced. Local content rules are the best tool for reducing U.S. auto imports in the 1990s. Increasing local content requirements will accelerate the transfer of "lean" production technology to the U.S. We should also require transplant firms to hire and train an increasing share of domestic workers as managers in these facilities. Such measures have been used in Canada and developing countries for many years to enhance the diffusion of new technology. U.S. policymakers should work from the premise that our production technology is no longer state-of-the-art in this industry.

In September, 1993 the Clinton Administration announced a new joint venture with the auto industry to develop a "supercar." This project is designed to develop a new lightweight, high-efficiency vehicle which will get 60 to 80 miles per gallon and have a low-polluting engine. It is designed as a cooperative effort in industrial policy that will combine resources from the national laboratories and all three U.S. firms in a concept based on the Apollo and Manhattan projects.[18] While this project may yield important results in the next decade, it is unlikely to solve the industry's twin structural problems: falling market share and outdated manufacturing technology.

The U.S. auto industry faces a new threat in the coming decade. The industry's recent recovery, including that of Ford and Chrysler, has been based on the rapid growth of truck demand. This recovery is extremely fragile. Any rapid escalation in the price of energy, or restriction in oil availability, will rapidly increase demand for small cars, as we observed on two occasions in the 1970s. The increasing reliance of U.S. vehicle producers on truck sales makes low energy prices an absolute necessity. An interesting irony of this strategy is that it contributes to future weakening of the U.S. trade account, because the U.S. has a large trade deficit in petroleum products, and because increases in the truck population will lower the efficiency of the U.S. vehicle fleet.

Thus the unintended benefits of our trade and energy regulations--enhanced U.S. output of energy-inefficient trucks--will increase overall fuel consumption, and the benefits may prove to be short-lived. The best way to improve fuel economy is to increase energy prices. Before that option is pursued, however, the U.S. needs to develop trade and industrial policies which give us the capacity to produce fuel-efficient autos, in this country. We should be able to identify reasonable long-run goals, including greater fuel efficiency, balanced trade and maintenance of a high-wage employment base, and identify a limited number of policies to achieve these goals. Continued inattention to these long-run goals is sure to result in declining employment, worsening of our trade balance and continued decay in this core sector of the economy. If we wait to pursue such policies until the next crisis is upon us, then we are sure to develop another round of short-sighted solutions.

NOTES

1. *Automotive News*, October 11, 1993, p. 37. These figures underestimate the total Japanese share of the U.S. vehicle market because they exclude captive imports--vehicles produced by Japanese firms but sold in the U.S. under the nameplates of U.S.-based automakers. In 1991, 2.1% of all vehicles sold in the U.S. were captive imports from Japan (1992 Wards Automotive Yearbook, p. 212).

2. See p. 29 and note 27 in chapter II for discussion of the truck tariff.

3. See p. 29 and note 26 in chapter II.

4. In April 1992 Japan announced that it was unilaterally tightening the VRA from 2.3 million units to 1.65 million for its 1993 fiscal year. Total imports from Japan have been less than the VRA ceiling since 1976 because of the growth in transplant production in North America and the devaluation of the U.S. dollar. 1.73 million cars were imported from Japan in their 1992 fiscal year. (Stokes, 1992, p. 474).

5. *Automotive News*, January 11, 1993, p. 51.

6. Council of Economic Advisors, *Economic Report of the President*, 1993, p. 470.

7. Imported and domestically produced vehicles are also treated as separate fleets under the CAFE rules, as discussed on pp. 75-77 in chapter V.

8. Brown, Warren, "The Great CAFE Caper; Automakers Find Ingenious Ways to Manipulate Federal Fuel Economy Rules,", *The Washington Post*, June 9, 1991, p. H1.

9. *Automotive News*, October 11, 1993, p. 37.

10. Anon. "A New Export Power in the Auto Industry? It's North American." *The Wall Street Journal*, October 18, 1993, p. A1.

11. The domestic price series in Figure 3 is highly correlated with the average wholesale price of autos used in this study. However, import prices at the port of entry (unit values), which are used in this study, diverge sharply from transaction prices because of dealer markup, changes in distributor markup and optional equipment added in this country.

12. *Citibase.* Data reported are for total employment in Standard Industrial Classification 371, motor vehicles and parts. Some auto parts are also produced in other industries (e.g. tires and glass).

13. Japanese producers have maintained their cost advantage over U.S. producers despite the devaluation of the U.S. dollar through domestic productivity improvements, by outsourcing of components to other Asian suppliers which have not experienced devaluation against the U.S. Dollar (e.g. Taiwan and some of the ASEAN countries) and by tolerating lower rates of return on their own capital. Prestowitz, *et al.* claim that "Over the past five to seven years, the Japanese auto companies, as a whole, have made money only on their sales in Japan." Note that this statement implies that Japanese producers have been dumping vehicles in the U.S.

14. Womack included Chrysler in the lean production category after the release of Womack *et al.* (1991). See Sawyer, Christopher A., "Womack's World", *Automotive Industries*, 172(7), July 1992, p. 32.

15. Womack, *et al.* (1991), pp 256-259.

16. Local content measures are generally combined with limits on imports. Vehicles exceeding the local content hurdle are then exempted from the import limit. Such measures have been implemented by the European Community, with local content requirements in excess of 80%.

17. U.S. Dept. of Commerce, *National Trade Data Bank*, 1993. These figures refer only to net imports in S.I.T.C. 87, Motor Vehicles and Parts. Vehicle parts in other import categories, including tires, radios and air conditioning parts totaled at least $1 billion in 1992.

18. Samuelson, Robert J. "Selling Supercar", *The Washington Post*, October 13, 1993, p. A21.

ACKNOWLEDGMENTS

During the course of this research I have benefitted from the advice, support and encouragement of many individuals and organizations. At the University of California at Berkeley, Professor Theodore E. Keeler, who served as my major advisor on this project, was a constant source of inspiration and support, and was particularly helpful in thinking through the relationships between the price, output and factor cost models. Professor Laura D'Andrea Tyson, one of the founders of the Berkeley Roundtable on International Economy (BRIE), provided the initial question which formed the basis for this research, as well as continuing feedback and encouragement. Professor John Zysman helped focus my research on public policy issues in this project and in several others that he supervised at BRIE, as well. I also benefitted from comments received and discussions with Professors Jeffrey Frankel, Richard Gilbert and David J. Teece. Dr. Janet Ceglowski also provided invaluable support and encouragement. I am indebted to several institutions for intellectual and financial support in this project.

The BRIE group provided an intellectual home, as well as a frame of reference, for this project. Prof. Stephen Cohen, co-director of BRIE, was a valued advisor. Fellow graduate students at BRIE, including Barbara Baran, Carol Parsons and Jay Stowsky were involved in several projects which contributed to this research, including one for the Congressional Office of Technology assessment which provided support for the literature review in chapter II. I have also received invaluable staff support from Ann Mine, Jay Tharp and several others at BRIE. Financial support was also received from the U.S. Dept. of Education and the Carnegie Corporation of New York, through BRIE.

This project continued under the support of a Herman Kahn Fellowship which I received from the Hudson Institute of Indianapolis, Indiana. In particular, I learned a great deal about applied empirical research and analysis from my fellow economists there, Dr. Richard W. Judy, Dr. David Reed, Dr. Jim Wheeler and Dr. David Weinschrott, and I also appreciate the support and encouragement of Neil Pickett and the rest of the officers and staff at the Hudson Institute.

This project was completed at the University of Maryland at College Park, where I benefitted greatly from the patience and encouragement of my colleagues. In particular I would like to thank my Chairman, Professor Thomas M. Corsi, and Professors Martin E. Dresner, Curtis M. Grimm, Richard Poist, Lee E. Preston, Carl A.

Scheraga and Robert J. Windle for their guidance, friendship and patience in listening to various pieces of and problems with this research. I would also like to thank Odell Frett, Donna Sabino and Eileen Spear for help with data acquisition, and Professor Daniel J. Power, Jeanne M. Fineran and the other staff members of the Office of Computing Services in the College of Business and Management for computer support. I also gratefully acknowledge support received from the Computer Science Center at the University of Maryland.

Finally, I wish to thank my wife Jenny and my daughters Carrie and Emma for their support, encouragement and tolerance of the long and difficult process of writing this book, and for accepting my many extended absences with love and good humor. Of course the views expressed in this work and the responsibility for any errors or omissions it may contain are mine, alone, and should not be ascribed to any of the individuals or organizations who have supported this project.

Short-Sighted
Solutions

CHAPTER I
INTRODUCTION

The U.S. auto industry has struggled for the past fifteen years. The oil price shocks of the 1970s led to increased demand for small, efficient cars which domestic firms were unable to sell at their usual rate of profit. They have found it difficult to counter the competitive success and rapid market share growth of Japanese small car makers. Environmental, safety and fuel economy regulations have significantly increased the cost of building and operating cars sold in the U.S. and have profoundly changed the strategies of domestic auto producers. As a result of these pressures, the U.S. auto industry has experienced steadily rising imports, declining industry employment and periodic profit crises in the 1970s and 1980s.

Despite these problems the domestic industry remains strong, although it no longer dominates the U.S. market. U.S. manufacturers have faced little competition in large car markets, except for the most expensive luxury vehicles. They possess distribution and service networks and established reputations which will make it difficult for newcomers to penetrate large car markets. Furthermore, U.S. automakers are earning substantial profits, and have the financial and technological ability to adapt rapidly to changing market conditions, as shown by the recent introduction of several successful new car models.

While the outlook for U.S.-based producers may be favorable, prospects for domestic employment opportunities are less sanguine. The literature reviewed in Chapter II shows that the growth of automotive imports over the past 15 years has significantly eroded job opportunities. In the future, U.S. firms must respond to the competitive threat posed by Asian based producers--who developed the ability in the late 1970s to build equivalent (or better) small cars at a lower cost than U.S. firms--if they are to avoid further loss of market share and profits. While all of the ways in which domestic firms can adapt will reduce

3

total labor demand in this sector, employment losses can be minimized by increasing the competitiveness of domestic assemblers and parts supplying industries. Offshoring of parts production, direct foreign investment by Japanese assemblers, and direct importing of cars by U.S. firms will all result in greater employment losses in the U.S. auto industry than would occur if production were retained in more efficient domestic firms.

In response to the rapid growth of imports and the loss of domestic jobs in this industry, the U.S. opted for trade protection in the early 1980s. The Japanese government agreed to a series of "Voluntary Restraint Agreements" (VRAs) which limited their auto exports to the U.S., and the U.S. government also imposed a substantial tariff increase on Japanese small pickups. The literature shows that while these policies did reverse the industry's profit slump in the early 1980s, they were also very costly for consumers. In addition, this study will show that trade protection did not substantially improve the long-run competitiveness of U.S. auto producers, and it also helped other foreign producers increase their penetration of the U.S. market.[1] An effective trade policy would have taken into account the effects of the oligopoly structure of the industry, the role of its trade union, and the special characteristics of production technology in this sector. This study will show that the VRAs, which lacked any of these collateral features, did little to improve the competitiveness of the domestic industry.

A. An Alternative Policy Approach: The Stakeholder Model

In order to be more effective, trade policy for the auto industry would have had to take into account the fact that there are a number of constituent groups who are both affected by and simultaneously determine the competitiveness of the domestic auto industry. The stakeholder model (Freeman and Gilbert, 1978) provides a convenient framework for analyzing the relationships between and interests of the various parties in this industry. It can also be used to suggest the outlines for a more comprehensive policy to help the industry resolve its competitive problems.

At the outset it is important to state that trade protection for the auto industry should be designed to improve the competitiveness of domestic producers. It is assumed that this is politically and socially desirable because it will help maintain employment levels in this high wage sector and in the many industries and communities which depend on it. In order to become more competitive, domestic producers would have to resist the temptation to earn excessive profits through unnecessary price increases.

This study will show that domestic firms were unwilling or unable to competitively price on their own under the VRAs. U.S. automakers used the VRAs to raise prices in all size classes of cars considered here (small, medium and large). This observation suggests that price restraint under trade protection would only have been possible if it had been enforced by a public agreement between the industry and the government which included price restraint standards and enforceable penalties for non-compliance.

An effective agreement would have included organized labor, a major stakeholder in this industry, in the bargaining process and would have incorporated incentives to raise productivity levels and improve the quality of domestic products. One important way to improve productivity and quality levels is to bring labor and management together to work out strategies for reorganizing production, eliminating arbitrary job definitions and incorporating new technologies in the most effective ways possible. Organization is the critical component of this process. Many studies have shown that the Japanese productivity advantage is the result of new or better ways of arranging production, rather than deeper capital investment or more sophisticated production technology. Historical prohibitions on labor participation in production management have limited the rate at which new forms of organization have been adopted in the U.S. auto industry.

The VRAs did not include mechanisms to encourage price or profit restraint on the part of the domestic producers or to bring together the participants in the industry in cooperative efforts to improve competitiveness. An effective trade policy would have required commitments from each stakeholder in the industry. Each would have been required to make sacrifices for the common good of the industry. Auto workers might have accepted a cut in their real wages, if they knew that the industry was also going to reduce profits and that salaried workers and management were also going to accept wage reductions[2]. They might have agreed to further cuts in the numbers of job categories if there were a joint plan for reducing employment through attrition, or enticing workers to leave through more effective job-training programs. Incentives for productivity improvement would have been larger if significant profit sharing at all firms had included production workers, and not just management employees.

With the rise in imports which occurred in 1985 and 1986, as the VRAs were relaxed and the Newly Industrializing Country (NIC) producers entered the market, the pressure for renewed import protection for the auto industry increased. Furthermore, as a result of the VRAs, Japanese and Korean producers have made commitments to dramatically expand their auto production facilities in North America.

These producers had plans to assemble 2.5 million units per year in the U.S. and Canada (United Auto Workers, 1987) by 1990. Most of these vehicles will be sold in the U.S., and thus it is likely that import nameplates will increase their share of the 15 million cars and trucks sold in the U.S. in 1987 (a good year) from 31% to 40% or even 45%.[3] This increase in transplant production will probably reduce the output and profits of the U.S.-based producers and total employment levels in the domestic auto assembly and parts industries.[4] These changes will, in turn, result in increased pressures for further protection of the domestic auto industry. The next round of public policies for this industry will be more effective if the stakeholders in the industry are required to make sacrifices and allowed to participate in the policy-making process.

B.   Domestic Employment and Oligopoly Behavior in the U.S. Auto Industry

Crandall (1984, 1986), the U.S. International Trade Commission (1985a) and several other authors have examined the effect of the VRAs on output, employment, and the prices paid by consumers for cars in the U.S. These studies all suffer from inadequate microeconomic models of the oligopolistic behavior of U.S. producers and the dynamic production strategies of the Japanese auto industry, and thus underestimate the effects of the VRAs on output and employment. The U.S. International Trade Commission, for example, simply estimated a logarithmic time-trend of the Japanese share of the U.S. market for the years 1967-80, and extrapolated this curve through 1984 to estimate potential Japanese market share without the VRAs.

A logarithmic time-trend underestimates the effect of the VRAs on Japanese market share because it does not reflect the capacity expansion plans and dynamic market-growth strategies of the Japanese firms. Crandall and the U.S. International Trade Commission were primarily concerned with the effects of the VRAs on the prices paid by consumers. A model based on modern oligopoly theory is developed in this study which yields more reliable estimates of the supply-side effects of the VRAs on both prices and output in the U.S. auto market. The employment displacement that would have resulted in the U.S. without the VRAs is estimated from projections of output, using a counterfactual simulation. Saving U.S. jobs was a major objective of the VRAs. The approach developed here will yield new and more accurate estimates of the number of jobs saved.

The first objective of this research is to develop a microeconomic model of firm behavior and market structure in the U.S. auto industry in order to derive more reliable estimates of the output effects of the

VRAs. It is necessary to account for the market power of domestic and foreign producers when projecting market shares if trade restraints had not been enacted. The second objective of this research is to estimate what effects alternative trade policies would have had on the competitiveness, output and employment of the U.S. auto industry.

A simultaneous equations model of supply and demand in the U.S. auto market (excluding the light-truck sector) is developed and estimated which explicitly accounts for: the variety of products available (through an estimate of the residual demand curve facing individual firms); the costs of production; and the effects of oligopoly behavior on firm supply and market output. Estimated parameters are used to predict changes in foreign and domestic market shares for the U.S. market under several counterfactual simulations.

This study makes several contributions to the economic literature. The model developed here complements Grossman's (1982 and 1984) pioneering empirical work on the effects of trade on employment and wages in perfectly competitive industries by establishing a parallel approach that can be used for oligopolistic industries. A new model of oligopoly behavior in industries with extensive product differentiation, developed by Baker and Bresnahan (1985a and 1985b), is used to analyze conditions in the domestic auto industry and the effects of trade policy.

Chapter II summarizes the economic conditions in the U.S. motor vehicle industry which led the government to provide trade protection for it in the early 1980s and reviews the literature on the impacts of the VRAs in particular. Chapter III reviews the literature on the empirical modeling of oligopoly power and specifies a particular reduced form model which is used here to estimate the impacts of the VRAs on the U.S. auto industry. Chapter IV describes the data sources used to estimate the model and summarizes some of the new data developed for this research. The model developed in Chapter III is estimated in Chapter V, and the effects of oligopoly structure on the performance of the domestic industry, as reflected in the estimates, are assessed. The model is then used to simulate the effects of the VRAs on output and prices in the U.S. auto market (vis-a-vis the alternative of no trade protection) in Chapter VI, and the employment effects of the VRAs are then estimated. The implications of this research for future trade and industrial policies for the U.S. auto industry are then discussed in Chapter VII.

NOTES

1.   Korean auto producers, in particular, benefitted greatly from the VRAs by forming alliances with Japanese and U.S. based assembly firms to rapidly expand their domestic auto industry and begin a major program of auto exports to the U.S. and other developed countries. Auto production and export was also stimulated in Mexico, Yugoslavia and Brazil by some of the same factors that helped the Koreans.

2.   The models estimated in Chapter V show that the VRAs had no significant effect on the total real costs of UAW labor.

3.   15.2 million vehicles (autos and light trucks) were sold in the U.S. in the calendar year of 1987. Of these, 4 million were imported and an additional 613,000 units were import nameplate vehicles assembled in the U.S., for a total import share of the U.S. market of 30.6% (Wards Communications Inc., 1988). If Transplant sales rose to 2.5 million units, with no reduction in direct imports, then the total import nameplate share would rise to 43% of U.S. sales, at this level of total demand.

The model developed in this study (Chapters III-VII) covers only auto sales. 10.3 million autos were sold in the U.S. in 1987. Of these, 3.2 million were imported and an additional 534,000 units were import nameplate cars assembled in the U.S., for a total import share of the U.S. car market of 36.3% (Wards Communications Inc., 1988).

4.   The UAW estimates that U.S. parts production for a vehicle assembled in a transplant facility requires only about 27% of the labor required to build a similar unit in a U.S. owned plant, because of the high level of imported parts (lower level of domestic content) used in such plants (UAW 1987).

CHAPTER II
BACKGROUND AND LITERATURE REVIEW

The world auto industry is a huge, complex system undergoing continuous evolution. In the past two decades the forces which are transfiguring the industry--changes in technology, patterns of demand, relative international competitiveness and government policies--have generated a rapid shift in the locations of production of still uncertain outcome, which is referred to by Altshuler as the fourth industrial transformation in the auto industry.[5] This chapter will analyze some of the most important trends affecting the U.S. auto industry and will then review the current literature on the effects of the VRAs on product quality, prices, output and employment in the domestic auto industry.

The chapter begins with a review of the structure of the domestic industry. Recent changes in patterns of demand and the competitiveness of the domestic producers, vis-a-vis their principal competitors in Japan, are examined in Section B. Several studies of the effects of trade on employment are critiqued in Section C. The chapter closes with a review of the literature on the particular effects of the VRAs on the U.S. auto industry, as a preface for a new analysis of this issue in the remainder of this study.

This chapter will review trends and conditions in the U.S. motor vehicle industry as a whole (that is--the market for both cars and light-trucks), while the remainder of this study (Chapters III-VII) will restrict its attention to the U.S. auto industry.

A. The Structure of the U.S. Motor Vehicle Industry

Direct employment in motor vehicle assembly and parts production reached an all-time peak in 1978 of 1,123,000 persons,[6] 5.5% of total manufacturing employment (U.S. Department of Labor 1985a). Approximately 2 indirect job opportunities are created for each person employed in the motor vehicle industry (U.S. Department of Labor 1985b). Thus more than 3 million people were directly and indirectly employed in the U.S. in the production of new vehicles in 1978. Direct employment in the industry fell to fewer than 800,000 persons in 1982, and then recovered to 982,000 in 1985. A steep, secular decline in employment began in the late 1970s. Total direct employment grew by about 1.5% between 1973 and 1978, but declined about 12% between 1978 and 1985 (all cyclical peaks).

The industry is heavily unionized, and workers are comparatively well paid. In 1983 production worker average hourly earnings were $12.12, 37 percent above the average manufacturing wage in that year (U.S. Department of Labor 1985a). If benefits are included in the calculation, the disparity is even larger. Total compensation per hour was $19.02 in the motor vehicle industry, about 55% higher than the manufacturing average (Crandall 1984).

Hourly earnings in the auto industry were rising between 1970 and 1977, both in real terms and relative to the manufacturing average. Between 1977 and 1984 real earnings were quite stable, averaging about $11.75 per hour (in real 1982 dollars). Average real earnings in the manufacturing sector were also stationary over this period, so the ratio of auto to manufacturing wages was essentially constant throughout the 1977-1984 period.

Some authors (i.e. Kreinen 1984) tend to focus exclusively on high production worker wages as the cause of the auto industry's competitive problems. However, the following analysis of the Manufacturing Cost Differential between U.S. and Japanese auto producers (the MCD) suggests that a number of factors contributed to the domestic industry's cost problems, including white collar wage rates, productivity levels, materials costs and quality problems. In 1979, when Japanese car sales were growing most rapidly, their average small car retail list price was $750 higher than that of domestic small cars. Costs (and wages) were not the only factor in the success of Japanese imports.

Vehicle production has historically been concentrated in the Great Lakes region of the country, with a few assembly plants located on the east and west coasts. However, in recent years most of the west coast plants have closed and a few plants have opened in the south. Even within these regions, production is concentrated within just a few states. Half of all U.S. employment in vehicle assembly in 1984 was located in the state of Michigan. Seventy percent of employment in this sector was located in just four states (Michigan, Missouri, Ohio and Wisconsin).[7] As the fortunes of the domestic auto industry have declined, these states have been particularly hard hit.

Employment in domestic vehicle production depends on overall levels of auto demand, the shares of domestic producers in U.S. and world markets (and recently, on the amount of U.S. production by foreign-owned firms), and trends in the structure of the production process. The structure of the U.S. motor vehicle market and its implications for conduct and performance in this sector will be considered next. Section B will consider some of the other factors which determine market shares and firm behavior in the domestic motor vehicle market.

1. Oligopoly Power in the U.S. Motor Vehicle Industry

While it has long been recognized that the high degree of concentration among U.S. car and truck producers is an important determinant of pricing and product characteristics in the industry (White, 1971), relatively little attention has been paid to the influence of oligopoly structure on the international competitive position of the U.S. motor vehicle industry. Most of the recent research on the competitive problems of the domestic industry has addressed the production cost advantage that has been secured (and expanded) by Japanese vehicle producers over the last ten years, and on the role of public policy in Japan (as executed by the Ministry of International Trade and Industry--MITI) in the creation of a more efficient vehicle production system (See Toder, 1978; Abernathy, Harbour and Henn, 1981; Flynn, 1982; Altshuler, *et al*, 1984; and Cole and Yakushiji, 1984). One recent article (Kwoka, 1984) does suggest that the rise in Japanese market share, and perhaps even the development of their production cost advantage, is the logical result of profit maximizing behavior under the prevailing market structures of the U.S. and Japanese motor vehicle industries. U.S. auto production has been dominated by 3 large firms in the post-war era. In contrast, there have been at least 8 Japanese auto producers serving a domestic market about half as large as the U.S. market, for most of this period.

Kwoka argues that the theory of dynamic limit pricing provides at least a partial explanation for the growth of small car imports into the U.S. Dynamic limit pricing suggests that an oligopolist with a large market share, and little or no cost advantage, will maximize profits by raising prices (thus allowing entry) to capture monopoly profits in the short run.[8] Kwoka also argues that concentration in the U.S. auto industry is responsible for the "quality gap" between U.S. and Japanese cars. In a market dominated by replacement demand, profits are maximized by increasing the rate of replacement of autos through frequent style changes and "planned obsolescence". Kwoka presents a theoretical argument and anecdotal evidence which suggests that "oligopolists' preference for style competition over more fundamental improvements" necessarily led to lower quality autos from Detroit, and conversely that Japanese auto production in a more competitive market, less dominated by replacement demand, resulted in better quality autos.

B.   Shifting Patterns of Vehicle Demand and Rising Imports

The U.S. motor vehicle market is the largest in the world. Despite the effects of the energy and environmental crises the U.S. auto market was stable or growing in the 1970s and 1980s. The future pattern of demand for autos, a critical determinant of output and employment in the domestic industry, has been the subject of several recent studies.[9] The consensus view is that on average the number of vehicles sold in the U.S. will exhibit a constant or rising trend in the future. This chapter analyzes the markets for both cars and trucks because small trucks (the bulk of all trucks sold) are close substitutes for cars, use many common parts and are produced by the same industry. The number of new vehicles (cars + trucks) sold appears to have leveled off in recent years, averaging 13.4 million units per year over the 1974-78 business cycle and only 12.9 million over the 1979-86 cycle. However, the industry encountered a set of unique problems in this period.[10] Altshuler, *et al* suggest that on average the number of vehicles sold will exhibit a constant or increasing trend in the future.

Although the average size of the domestic market for new vehicles has shown no significant trend over the past 15 years, domestic producers have been losing market share in the 1970s and 1980s for several reasons. First, the energy price shocks of 1973 and 1979 increased the demand for small, fuel efficient vehicles. Between 1970 and 1973, the small car share of the number of autos sold in the U.S. averaged 30.8%.[11] From 1974 to 1976, following the first oil crisis, the small car share rose to an average of 43.5%. From 1976 to 1978, the years preceding the second round of OPEC oil price increases, the average small car share remained roughly constant at 43.9%. Higher gasoline prices then sent the small car share up to 55.8% over the 1979-81 period. With the decline in gasoline prices in the early 1980s the share of small cars declined to about 50%.

The Japanese share of the U.S. auto market, shown in Figure 1, increased with each jump in gasoline prices. Between 1970 and 1973 Japanese auto imports, all small cars, averaged 6.1% of the total U.S. market. After the 1973 oil embargo, their share rose to 9.3% between 1974 and 1976. Their share growth continued between 1976 and 1978, when Japanese firms average market share was 12.5%. The growth in Japanese imports then accelerated after the second oil price hike to average 20.0% between 1979 and 1981. After 1980 Japanese vehicle exports to the U.S. were limited by U.S. trade restraints. Thus, the

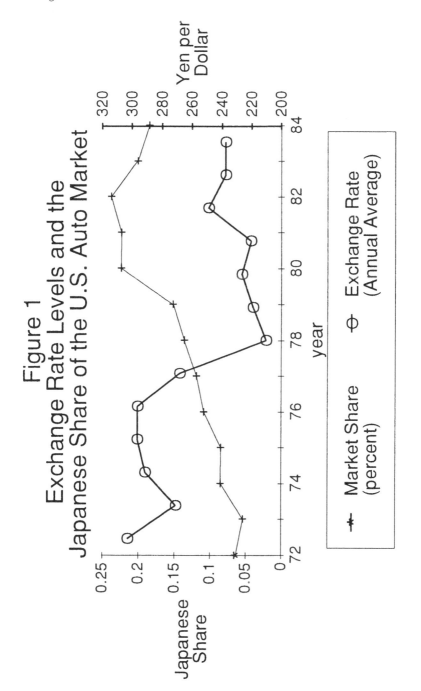

Figure 1
Exchange Rate Levels and the
Japanese Share of the U.S. Auto Market

growth of Japanese imports is at least partially explained by the shift in demand patterns to small cars. However, import share data also suggest that several other factors were at work.

First, note that the market share of Japanese firms increased substantially during the 1976-78 period, when there was no appreciable growth in the overall share of small car sales. Furthermore, Figure 1 shows that during this period the dollar lost about one third of its value against the yen, raising the delivered cost of Japanese imports. It is also informative to compare Japanese import performance during the two large upswings in small car demand, after the oil price shocks of the 1970s. After 1973 the small car share grew by 12.7 percentage points. Japanese imports captured about one quarter of this share growth. After 1978 the small car share grew by 11.9 percentage points. Japanese imports captured about two thirds of the share growth in the later period. Finally, in 1980 Japanese firms planned to increase motor vehicle assembly capacity by an additional 20% through 1983, enough capacity to double their share of the U.S. market in the early 1980s, a period when gasoline prices and the market share of small cars were stable or declining. These observations suggest that Japanese firms had achieved a substantial competitive advantage over U.S. firms by the late 1970s.

Another indication of the competitiveness of Japanese auto makers is the fact that their share of the world auto market rose substantially during the 1970s (while the U.S. share fell). In the 1980s, however, almost all European countries also imposed formal or informal restrictions on Japanese vehicle imports, limiting further growth in their share of the world market, at least through exports from their home base.

The Japanese also achieved rapid share growth in the U.S. small truck market in the 1970s, which was expanding rapidly at the time, displacing additional domestic labor. 19.4% of the number of vehicles sold in the U.S. in 1972 were trucks. The truck share rose to 26.8% in 1978 and before falling to 20.0% in 1980. The decline in the truck share is largely explained by the 1979 shift in gasoline prices, and by a 1980 customs ruling which reclassified most Japanese small truck imports (which were then imported as separate chassis cabs and cargo bodies) as finished trucks subject to an existing 25% tariff. In 1972, imports accounted for 12.7% of the number of trucks sold in the U.S. In 1980, before the customs ruling, the import share had risen to 33.6%. Following the truck tariff ruling the import share of the U.S. truck market declined to 25.8% in 1984 and 17.3% in 1987. The share of trucks in total demand grew in the 1980s, to about 33% in 1987 (Wards

Communications Inc. 1988), as domestic producers introduced new models and real gasoline prices declined.

1. Recent Import Trends

Even though overall vehicle demand remained firm, the U.S. industry was losing employment and market share to imports throughout the 1970s. Tables 1 and 2 summarize recent trends in motor vehicle trade. Several tendencies in these data stand out. First, it is clear that net trade (in terms of both units and the value of sales) is consistently negative and increasing in magnitude, so trade has reduced the number of domestic job opportunities. The import share of the number of vehicles sold (Table 1), is higher in every year than the import share of the value of sales (Table 2), in part, because the average import was cheaper than the average domestic vehicle. U.S. producers perform better in the larger, more expensive model lines. However, over this period import prices appear to be catching up with domestic models. The number of vehicles imported from all sources grew 77% between 1970 and 1980, while the import share of the value of the domestic market increased 128%.

TABLE 1

U.S. Motor Vehicle Trade: Quantities Exchanged and
Shares of Apparent Domestic Consumption, 1970-1988
(thousands of units)

Apparent Domestic Consumpt.		German Impts.		Japanese Impts.		All Sources of Imports		NetTrade	
Year	Units	Units	Share	Units	Share	Units	Share	Units	Share
1970	10,002	675	6.7%	409	4.1%	2,180	21.8%	-1,795	-17.9%
1971	12,941	771	6.0%	788	6.1%	2,825	21.8%	-2,337	-18.1%
1972	13,518	677	5.0%	857	6.3%	2,818	20.8%	-2,282	-16.9%
1973	14,704	677	4.6%	785	5.3%	2,764	18.8%	-2,103	-14.3%
1974	12,183	620	5.1%	1,034	8.5%	2,974	24.4%	-2,162	-17.8%
1975	10,448	370	3.5%	837	8.0%	2,369	22.7%	-1,503	-14.4%
1976	13,586	350	2.6%	1,385	10.2%	3,024	22.3%	-2,143	-15.8%
1977	15,020	423	2.8%	1,570	10.5%	3,319	22.1%	-2,412	-16.1%
1978	15,718	416	2.6%	1,931	12.3%	3,768	24.0%	-2,882	-18.3%
1979	14,135	496	3.5%	2,015	14.3%	3,683	26.1%	-2,711	-19.2%
1980	11,130	339	3.0%	2,474	22.2%	3,864	34.7%	-3,097	-27.8%
1981	10,866	234	2.2%	2,367	21.8%	3,589	33.0%	-2,910	-26.8%
1982	10,073	259	2.6%	2,157	21.4%	3,624	36.0%	-3,145	-31.2%
1983	12,420	240	1.9%	2,302	18.5%	3,945	31.8%	-3,293	-26.5%
1984	14,543	335	2.3%	2,515	17.3%	4,587	31.5%	-3,847	-26.5%
1985	16,135	473	2.9%	3,331	20.6%	5,561	34.5%	-4,713	-29.2%
1986	16,032	452	2.8%	3,595	22.4%	5,956	37.2%	-5,114	-31.9%
1987	15,771	378	2.4%	3,190	20.2%	5,600	35.5%	-4,788	-30.4%
1988	N/A	264	N/A	2,671	N/A	5,300	N/A	-4,337	N/A

Sources: U.S.I.T.C. 1985c; and U.S.I.T.C, The U.S. Automobile Industry: Monthly Report on Selected Economic Indicators, (various issues).

Important country specific differences in import patterns are apparent in Tables 1 and 2, and in Figure 2 (U.S.-Canadian Vehicle trade). Imports from Japan grew consistently over the 1970-1980 period, in both unit and sales-value terms. Japanese sales in the U.S. exhibit less cyclical variability than overall domestic consumption. The average real unit value (actual wholesale values divided by the implicit price deflator for the U.S. Gross National Product, Table 2) of Japanese imports rose 28.8% over the 1972-80 period, versus 11.3% for all vehicles sold in the U.S. These data suggest that Japanese assemblers were moving into more expensive product lines in the U.S. market. This process was accelerated by the trade restraints imposed in the 1980s on Japanese vehicle exports to the U.S. Between 1980 and 1986 average unit value of Japanese imports rose 56% (in real terms).

TABLE 2

U.S. Motor Vehicle Trade: The Value of Sales and
Shares of Apparent Domestic Consumption, 1970-1988[12]
(millions of 1982 dollars[13])

Year	Apparent Domestic Consumpt. Value	German Impts. Value	German Impts. Share	Japanese Impts. Value	Japanese Impts. Share	All Sources of Imports Value	All Sources of Imports Share	Net Trade (X-M) Value	Net Trade (X-M) Share
1970	90,541	2,524	2.8%	1,085	1.2%	8,322	9.2%	-7,198	-8.0%
1971	107,658	2,878	2.7%	2,151	2.0%	12,584	11.7%	-9,347	-8.7%
1972	118,451	3,046	2.6%	2,700	2.3%	13,465	11.4%	-10,382	-8.8%
1973	125,328	3,640	2.9%	2,630	2.1%	13,980	11.2%	-10,242	-8.2%
1974	103,148	3,466	3.4%	3,198	3.1%	15,064	14.6%	-9,259	-9.0%
1975	99,536	2,544	2.6%	2,946	3.0%	13,575	13.6%	-5,734	-5.8%
1976	121,737	2,540	2.1%	5,949	4.9%	16,170	13.3%	-9,084	-7.5%
1977	137,755	3,311	2.4%	7,157	5.2%	18,244	13.2%	-11,334	-8.2%
1978	144,391	3,853	2.7%	7,995	5.5%	22,217	15.4%	-15,132	-10.5%
1979	134,108	4,061	3.0%	8,268	6.2%	20,828	15.5%	-13,395	-10.0%
1980	101,954	3,834	3.8%	10,040	9.8%	21,450	21.0%	-16,161	-15.9%
1981	102,262	2,793	2.7%	12,034	11.8%	22,792	22.3%	-16,316	-16.0%
1982	97,326	3,173	3.3%	11,084	11.4%	24,303	25.0%	-20,120	-20.7%
1983	117,309	3,301	2.8%	12,048	10.3%	26,890	22.9%	-22,388	-19.1%
1984	139,327	4,233	3.0%	13,642	9.8%	32,819	23.6%	-29,304	-21.0%
1985	151,284	5,608	3.7%	17,688	11.7%	38,596	25.5%	-33,123	-21.9%
1986	152,479	7,127	4.7%	22,782	14.9%	46,392	30.4%	-40,632	-26.6%
1987	142,511	7,565	5.3%	21,740	15.3%	46,339	32.5%	-41,130	-28.9%
1988	N/A	5,324	N/A	19,106	N/A	44,462	N/A	0	N/A

Sources: U.S.I.T.C.   1985c;   U.S.I.T.C,   *The   U.S.   Automobile Industry;   Monthly   Report   on   Selected   Economic Indicators*,   (various   issues);   and   Citibase,   "Citicorp Data Base Services".

German exports of cheap small cars to the U.S. (principally Volkswagens) were displaced by Japanese models in the 1970s. German firms successfully maneuvered the transition to higher-valued export cars in this period. The number of German vehicles sold in the U.S. market declined steadily throughout the 1970s and 1980s. However, the German share of the value of U.S. sales was roughly constant (Table 2). Thus average real unit values for German imports rose by 150% over 1972-80 and another 40% between 1980 and 1986.

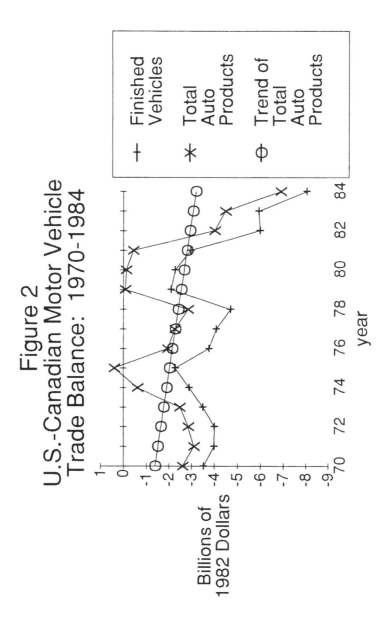

Figure 2
U.S.-Canadian Motor Vehicle
Trade Balance: 1970-1984

U.S.-Canadian vehicle trade involves a much larger amount of intra-industry product shipment than U.S.-German or U.S.-Japanese trade. In 1984 94% of all U.S. auto exports (in value terms) were sold to Canada. The U.S. and Canadian motor vehicle markets are almost completely integrated with production in both countries dominated by the major U.S.-based firms.[14] However, the U.S. ran a trade deficit with Canada on finished vehicles over the entire 1970-84 period (figure 2). This was partially offset by a positive trade balance on motor vehicle parts, but on the whole the U.S. trade balance on all motor vehicle products has generally been negative, and the bilateral deficit has followed an increasing trend in the last 10 years. Between 1976 and 1984 the Canadian dollar was steadily depreciating against the U.S. dollar, losing about one third of its value, thus lowering relative production costs in Canada for U.S.-based firms. U.S. firms responded to the lower value of the Canadian Dollar by moving a greater share of North American production to Canadian plants.

2. *The Japanese Cost Advantage*

There is wide agreement in the literature that U.S.-based firms could not produce small cars as cheaply as Japanese assemblers in the early 1980s. Toder (1978) estimated that the Japanese were almost cost-competitive with U.S. producers in 1973, for high volume production, and had a cost advantage for volumes of under 300,000 units per year of any particular sub-compact car. By 1979 the Japanese producers appear to have gained a $1500-$2000 per-unit cost advantage in subcompacts. By 1979 the quality of small cars sold by Japanese firms was higher than that of domestic small cars sold in the U.S. market. The prices of U.S. small cars were lower, on average, than Japanese small cars (Feenstra 1985a, 1985b) and yet domestic manufacturers were losing market share, because of the price/quality gap.

Fuss and Waverman (1986) present new estimates of the cost and efficiency differences between U.S. and Japanese producers, based on an econometric cost function model. They conclude that the MCD figures discussed above overestimate the Japanese cost advantage because they fail to correct for differences in capacity utilization in 1979-80 and for the undervaluation of the Yen. However, their analysis is based on highly aggregated data (3 digit S.I.C. level).

Aizcorbe, Winston and Friedlander (1987) developed the most fine-grained data set used to date for an econometric study of the costs of auto production in the U.S. and Japan, relying on a pooled cross-section, time series sample of firm-level data. They claim that U.S. and Japanese production costs would be equalized at an exchange rate of 151.9 yen per dollar. However, this estimate is based on a prediction from their model that U.S. small car production costs in 1982 equalled $3,336 per car, more than a thousand dollars less than their estimate for U.S. production costs in 1980 of $4,428 per car.

The model estimated by Aizcorbe, Winston and Friedlander assumed a trans-log cost function, and utilized annual data for the period 1958 to 1983 for U.S. firms (and 1970 to 1982 for Japanese firms). It is well known that translog estimates are reliable only in the vicinity of the sample means, and that the reliability of estimates decreases as estimates move towards or beyond sample limits. Furthermore, the levels of capacity utilization in the U.S. and Japanese auto industries were very different in 1982, because of the recession in the U.S. It is more appropriate to compare costs in periods when there were similar levels of capacity utilization in both industries. 1980 is a better year for making such a comparison. Aizcorbe, *et al,* estimated that the MCD was $2,369 in 1980 and $1,409 in 1982.

In view of the uncertainty inherent in estimates of the MCD, it seems more prudent to assume that the MCD in the early 1980s fell somewhere in the range of $1,409 to $2,369, rather than to rely on the point estimate from 1982 only. This is consistent with engineering based estimates of the MCD in the 1979-80 time period, which ranged between $1,304 and $2,489.[15] Under this assumption, the MCD would have been eliminated at an exchange rate somewhere in the range of 151.9 to 105.4 yen per dollar, assuming that changes in currency values had no effect on Yen-denominated production costs in Japan. This assumption probably overestimates the effects of exchange rate shifts on the delivered costs of Japanese manufacturers in the U.S., because "about 15% of the costs of manufacturing a Japanese vehicle is imported (Aizcorbe, *et al,* p.19, footnote 31)", and this proportion may have increased as the Yen appreciated (see note 20, below).

Thus the dollar may have to fall far below its 1989 level, in the range of 125 to 130 yen per dollar, in order to eliminate the MCD. Even if cost-parity were to be achieved, U.S. manufacturers would still face a substantial "quality gap" with their product offerings. U.S. auto makers continue to claim an efficiency disadvantage and to invest in new technology designed to overcome the Japanese MCD. Thus it is important to review the earlier engineering-based estimates of the MCD.

Cole and Yakushiji (1984) and Flynn (1982) review all published estimates of the size of the MCD in the 1979-1980 period. Their analysis covers ten estimates of the total *manufacturing cost* differential which report MCDs ranging from $1,304 to $2,489. Given an additional cost of $400 for tariff and transportation costs, the average *landed cost* advantage for Japanese producers for a standard subcompact is $1,468 in the 10 studies reviewed by Cole and Yakushiji. A recent set of estimates of the MCD is presented in Table 3.

TABLE 3

Estimates of U.S. and Japanese Manufacturing Costs
for a standard subcompact in 1979-1980[16]

(Costs Expressed in U.S. Dollars, assuming 210-215 Yen/Dollar)

cost component	Japanese cost	U.S. cost	cost difference
Labor costs[17]	878.33	2,310.91	1,432.58
Materials	2,143.67	2,969.88	826.21
Selling and advertising	556.00	427.25	-128.75
Capital	516.00	283.97	-232.03
Total manufacturing cost	4,094.00	5,992.01	1,898.01
Tariff and Transportation[18]	400.00	0.	-400.00
Total landed cost	4,494.00	5,992.01	1498.01

Source: Flynn, Michael S., "Differentials in Vehicles'
          Landed Costs: Japanese Vehicles in the U.S.
          Marketplace", Working Paper Series No. 3, (Ann
          Arbor, MI: Center For Japanese Studies,
          University of Michigan; October 30, 1982).

There have been extensive debates in the literature about the types of estimates shown in Table 3. The remainder of this section will: 1) analyze the components of the MCD, 2) discuss technical problems with its measurement, and 3) end with an assessment of the current state of the MCD.

a. Labor Costs. The labor cost factor in Table 3 has received the most attention. Labor costs are usually divided into two categories, differences in wage rates and differences in labor productivity. Flynn (1983) examined 4 of the MCD estimates referred to above and found that the proportion of the labor cost difference attributed to wage rates ranged from 26% to 60%, while the proportion attributed to labor productivity ranged from 18% to 74%.[19] Flynn noted that if wages are higher in the U.S., then the cost of lower U.S. labor productivity are greater than they would be if wages were the same in both countries (and vice versa). He suggests splitting labor costs into three components: wage costs, productivity costs and joint effects (wage differences times productivity differences), thus decomposing the variance in the estimates of the labor cost gap.[20] Flynn revised the labor cost breakdowns for the 4 MCD studies, and derived new estimates of the components of the labor cost gap which average 37% labor productivity, 36% wage rates and 27% joint effects, although there is still a wide disparity in these estimates among the individual studies.

Flynn's analysis suggests that labor productivity and wage rates are equally important determinants of the labor cost differential. Flynn (1984) also notes that the disparity between U.S. and Japanese white collar wages is greater than the wage difference for production workers, and as a result about half of the difference in compensation costs in 1980 could be attributed to white collar wages, while only one third of U.S. motor vehicle workers held white collar jobs. This illustrates the importance of separately considering blue and white collar labor costs.

b. Production Worker Wages. Real hourly earnings of U.S. production workers were constant between 1977 and 1984, as mentioned above. This section will compare *nominal* wage rates in U.S. and Japan, at various exchange rates, to evaluate relative wage levels in the two countries. Changes in the Yen/Dollar exchange rate and the use of profit sharing in the Japanese compensation system complicate comparisons of relative wages in the two countries. The U.S. Department of Labor estimated that in 1983 total hourly compensation (including fringe benefits) of U.S. auto workers was $19.02 per hour while their Japanese counterparts earned $7.91 (Crandall 1984). However, the average value of the dollar in 1983 was about 240 Yen. By April, 1987 the dollar had fallen to 145 Yen. At that rate, the comparative hourly costs would have been $19.02 (U.S.) and $13.09 (Japan) in 1983. By 1987 hourly costs had risen to roughly $23.00 in the U.S. and $16.50 in Japan.[21]

The U.S. Department of Labor apparently does not include profit sharing in its calculation of hourly compensation costs. Flynn (1984) provides a detailed breakdown for one Japanese producer who had a total hourly compensation of cost $10.80 in 1983 (at 240 Yen/Dollar). Profit sharing represented $2.57 and other direct and indirect payments equaled $8.23. The later figure is nearly identical to the U.S. Department of Labor total compensation estimate for that year ($7.91). Adding in profit sharing (at 145 Yen/Dollar) yields a complete estimate of comparative hourly compensation rates of roughly $23 in the U.S. and $21 in Japan. Hourly labor costs for production workers in 1987 would have been equal in the U.S. and in Japan at an exchange rate of 132 Yen per dollar, according to these estimates.

c. White Collar Labor Costs. The ratio of the wages of salaried employees to production workers is much higher in U.S. firms than in Japanese firms. As a result, the fall in the value of the dollar between 1985 and 1987 did not eliminate the white collar wage gap. In 1980, assuming 240 Yen per dollar, white collar compensation costs were $28.28 per hour in the U.S. and $12.00 per hour, including profit sharing, in Japan (Flynn 1984). At 145 Yen per dollar the Japanese white collar cost was $19.86. Salaried employees represent about one third of the labor going into an auto. In 1987 there was still a significant wage gap between U.S. and Japanese firms at the white collar level. The exchange rate would have had to fall to 102 Yen per dollar to close the estimated 1987 white collar wage-rate gap.

d. Other Cost Factors. The Japanese advantage in the cost of materials (Table 3) reflects both productivity and wage differences (Cole and Yakushiji 1984). The U.S. advantage in selling costs probably reflects scale economies in advertising.[22] Capital cost differences are at least partially explained by differences in rates of return in 1979-80 (a period of declining profits in the U.S. industry). The use of capital costs for a normal business year in the U.S. would probably increase estimated capital costs for domestic producers, and the estimated MCD.

e. Reliability of the MCD Estimates. There are at least three fundamental problems with the kinds of estimates shown in Table 3. The first issue is the way in which exchange rate fluctuations affect relative production costs. The Yen/Dollar rate has varied widely in recent years from the 210-215 level used in Table 3, as shown in Figure 1. If it is assumed that all Japanese production and delivery costs listed in Table 3 are paid in Yen, and that productivity and domestic currency costs remained at their 1980 levels, then estimated landed costs would be equal at an exchange rate of 159 Yen per U.S. Dollar. The fact that the Dollar was as low as 145 Yen by April 1987, would suggest that exchange rate movements had eliminated the MCD.[23] However, it appears that all Japanese production costs are not paid for in Yen, but that the Japanese obtain an increasing share of parts and materials from Taiwan and other countries whose currencies move with the dollar.[24] Thus, the MCD may have been reduced by recent exchange rate movements, but trends in product markets suggest that Japanese firms are still highly competitive in both price and quality terms with U.S. manufacturers.

A second general problem is that the database used for most engineering-based studies of the MCD is quite limited and has not been publicly evaluated. All of the analyses reviewed by Cole and Yakushiji are based on either private, firm specific data or a proprietary data set developed by Harbour. However, an MCD in the early 1980s which is similar to the estimate shown in Table 3 has been identified in an econometric cost study based on publicly available accounting data (Aizcorbe, Winston and Friedlander, 1987), as discussed above.

A third general problem with the literature on the MCD is that it ignores dynamic trends in production costs. Very little is known about trends in the fundamental determinants of the MCD, especially in labor productivity, since the early 1980s. Dynamic factors could increase or decrease the estimated MCD. Growth in the average age of Japanese auto workers could lead to rapid relative wage growth because there are strong seniority premia built into the Japanese wage structure. Productivity growth in the U.S. auto industry may have exceeded that in Japan in the past 6-7 years. However, Japanese producers may have gone further in sourcing components from low-wage NIC producers.

f. Manufacturing Costs in 1987. Despite the 1985-87 fall in the value of the dollar U.S. producers continued to claim an efficiency disadvantage and to pursue various options designed to improve their competitiveness including new technology, changes in the organization of production, changes in supplier relationships and new quality control methods. *Japanese producers probably possess some cost advantage over U.S. firms in 1989*, especially if the cost comparison is made for vehicles of similar "quality" levels. The wage gap has been reduced, but there is little evidence of enough productivity growth in the U.S. to close the gap in the number of hours it takes to build a typical small car. Japanese producers have diminished the effect of the dollar's fall by switching to suppliers in other countries with lower costs.

Even if costs were roughly comparable in the 1986-1987 period for small cars built by U.S.- and Japanese-based assemblers, U.S. producers still apparently faced a major *quality* gap. In the 1980s many U.S. consumers were willing to pay substantially more for Japanese cars than for comparable U.S. small cars. The Japanese share of the U.S. auto market rose in 1986 and 1987, despite dramatic increases in the value of the Yen and thus in the landed cost and prices of these imports.[25]

Recently new producers, based in Korea, have entered the U.S. market and have had very substantial rates of sales growth. Very little public information is available about the relative costs of Korean auto production. However, the prices of Korean-made cars have generally been lower than those of comparable models from U.S. producers. Domestic firms are now facing increased competition from Japanese firms turning out larger, more luxurious, high quality products and from new producers making low cost, low quality small cars for the U.S. market.

C. The Effects of Trade on Employment

The domestic motor vehicle industry was challenged by growing competitive problems in a number of market segments in the 1970s and

1980s. Rising imports significantly reduced employment opportunities in this sector. Several large recessions and price increases for new equipment needed to comply with government regulations also reduced demand for cars and trucks. Rising unemployment and declining profits in this period generated a debate on the industry's difficulties which is reviewed here. Two primary, inter-related issues are discussed. The first is the number of job opportunities eliminated in the U.S. by rising vehicle imports. The second is the relative importance of the effects of trade, and the effects of macroeconomic factors on job opportunities. These issues have been addressed in several input/output (or accounting-type) studies which are reviewed in this section.

In 1980 and 1981 the U.S. government responded to the auto industry's problems by imposing a large tariff on most Japanese truck imports (through an administrative measure) and by negotiating the VRAs with the Japanese government, which put a ceiling on auto exports to the U.S. These agreements were extended several times and remained in effect in 1989. There is an extensive debate about the effects of the VRAs on employment in and the competitiveness of the domestic auto industry in the 1980s. This discussion revolves around estimates of what domestic output and employment in the 1980s would have been without the VRAs. Section D critiques this literature, setting the stage for a new model of the effects of the VRAs on output, prices and employment in the U.S. auto industry which is developed in Chapters III through VII.

1. Estimates of the Effects of Trade on Employment

The U.S. trade deficit in motor vehicles was growing throughout the 1970s and early 1980s, as shown in Tables 1 and 2. There were fewer jobs available than there would have been if vehicle trade had been balanced. One input-output study suggests that between 1970 and 1980 there was an 11% decline in the number of domestic job opportunities (about 88,700 work years) because of the *increase* in net imports in this industry (Lawrence 1984). The U.S. International Trade Commission (USITC) found that if trade had been balanced in 1980, there would have been an additional 170,000 job opportunities in the motor vehicle industry, a 21% increase over actual employment levels in that year (USITC 1986).[26] Despite the effects of trade protection, the labor content of trade in the motor vehicle industry rose to 301,000 work-years in 1985.

a. Input-Output Studies. There are three measures of employment from trade which have been estimated using input-output techniques. The *direct* effect is the number of job opportunities which would have been preserved in the motor vehicle industries if imports had equaled exports in this sector (if trade were balanced). The second is the employment effect of motor vehicle trade in industries which supply parts and materials used to make cars, such as steel and tires (the *indirect* effect). The third type is an alternative way of calculating the indirect effects, which measures the impacts of trade flows in other industries on output and employment in autos (i.e. the effect of a decline in grain exports on the truck sales to grain farmers). Each type of indirect effect has been estimated in at least one of the studies reviewed below. This section will focus on the indirect effects of trade on employment in parts and materials supplier-industries because vehicle production is such an important source of demand for the products of these industries.

The input-output estimates discussed above include both direct and indirect effects of trade on vehicle industry employment. The USITC (1986) also separately estimated direct employment content of trade for the years 1978 through 1985, and estimated that 115,000 job opportunities (11.4% of industry employment) would have been created in 1978 if vehicle trade had been balanced. By 1980, this figure had risen to 125,000 work years, despite the fact that the value of total domestic auto consumption fell by almost one third between 1978 and 1980. In 1985 the employment effect of vehicle trade had risen to 219,000 work years, notwithstanding the effects of trade restraints. This is explained, in part, by a shift to higher valued Japanese auto imports which was caused by the VRAs.

An unpublished study from the U.S. Bureau of Labor Statistics can be used to estimate the indirect effects of trade on job opportunities in supplier industries. For each work year of labor content embodied in the products of the motor vehicle industry, 2 additional work years of employment are generated in supplier industries.[27] In 1978, in addition to the 115,000 work years of direct labor, 232,000 work years were embodied in the intermediate products displace by net vehicle imports. Thus the total (direct + indirect or supplier industry employment effects) labor content of vehicle trade in 1978 equaled 347,000 work years, or 39% of the labor content of all U.S. trade in 1978. This illustrates the major role played by motor vehicles in the U.S. trade deficit. By 1985 the total labor content of U.S. vehicle imports had risen to 661,000 work years, but the labor content of U.S. trade grew more rapidly, so the vehicle industry share fell to 24%.

b. Domestic Problems vs. Foreign Trade. One of the most widely quoted input-output studies of the effects of trade on employment is by Robert Lawrence (1984) of the Brookings Institution. His work casts doubt on the view that trade is deindustrializing the U.S. economy. Lawrence used an accounting framework to allocate changes in value added and employment in 52 manufacturing industries to changes in foreign trade and changes in patterns of domestic demand. Lawrence contends that structural change in employment and output patterns in the U.S. has been driven by changes in the patterns of domestic demand, and that growth in imports played a secondary role in that process. His conclusions are controversial.

Lawrence estimated the direct and indirect effects of trade on employment in vehicle production. He found that over the 1970s the auto industry was the only sector where "the employment decline was due to trade and that without trade, employment would have grown (Lawrence 1984, p. 60)." Between 1970 and 1980 (years with similar levels of capacity utilization) Lawrence found that total employment in motor vehicles and equipment fell by 1.3%, the sum of a 9.9% increase due to domestic demand and a 11.1% decline due to the change in foreign trade (88,700 work years).

Despite these results Lawrence still claims that "even in automobiles, problems stem from domestic sources (Lawrence 1984, p. 60)." He supports this claim by noting the large decline in U.S. vehicle output between 1973 and 1980. 1973 was a peak output year in autos, and in 1980 the industry was in the midst of a major recession. Lawrence found that between 1973 and 1980 employment fell by 19.2%, the sum of a 12.8% decrease due to domestic demand and a 6.4% decrease due to the change in foreign trade (about 62,500 work-years).

Lawrence's analysis of the 1973-1980 period is analytically flawed. By comparing the level of net trade in a boom year (1973) with trade in an extremely depressed year (1980) he overstates the importance of domestic demand in the industry's difficulties, and underestimates the effects of trade on employment, because the value of imports would have been much larger if 1980 had been a cyclical peak. The debates about the effects of trade on employment are concerned with long-term secular trends. When analyzing secular trends, the preferred approach is to compare cyclical peaks or average import levels over complete business cycles.

A constant share analysis is one way to correct for cyclical effects in order to compare two years with different levels of capacity utilization.[28] If the import share of the value of motor vehicle sales had remained constant between 1973 and 1980, then the employment content of trade would have been 87,400 work years lower than it actually was (versus Lawrence's estimate of 62,500).[29] The constant share approach suggests that trade was responsible for a 9.0% decrease in the demand for labor between 1973 and 1980, while domestic demand was responsible for a 10.2% decrease (compared with Lawrence's estimates of 6.4% and 12.8%, respectively). Thus, even over this recessionary period, trade appears to be about as important as domestic demand in explaining the decline in domestic auto industry employment.

c. Problems Common to Input-Output Studies. The input-output studies reviewed in this section suffer from the general flaws in accounting type models pointed out by Martin and Evans (1981), Grossman (1982), and by Dickens (1988). First, increased foreign competition can lead domestic producers to adopt new, labor displacing technologies, making it difficult to distinguish between the employment effects of trade and those of productivity growth. Second, the input-output approach also assumes that imported products are perfect substitutes for domestically produced goods, and that the "labor content of U.S. imports of a good are estimated to be the labor inputs that would be required to make the same dollar amount of the domestic substitute (USITC 1986)". However, domestic substitutes for imported cars would be more costly, per unit, because more labor is required to produce domestic small cars, and wages and the other components of auto production costs are higher in the U.S. than they are in Japan (as shown above). As a result, fewer cars would be sold in a protected domestic market (because prices would be higher), but more labor would be required to build each car. The input-output approach can overstate or understate the employment effects of trade, depending on the elasticity of market demand and the relative costs of domestic and foreign production.

Although the assumption that imports could be replaced with domestic substitutes of similar cost is not valid, there is another useful interpretation of the labor content estimates derived using the input-output approach. To the extent that the import problem in autos is a result of less efficient production technology in the domestic industry (rather than factor cost problems), these estimates can be interpreted as the employment cost of the technology gap between U.S. firms and foreign competitors. This appears to be an appropriate description of the situation in the 1970s, when significant growth in the share of small cars took place. Japanese producers had concentrated on efficient production of small cars for their home market, while U.S. producers lagged behind in small car production technology. Despite the problems discussed here input-output type measures provide the only complete estimates available of the employment content of trade in this period.

d. Exchange Rate Effects. A number of studies, discussed in previous chapters, have suggested that the competitive problems of U.S.

manufacturing industries in the early 1980s are simply the result of the rise in the dollar in this period. The auto industry's competitive problems began in the 1970s, before the dollar's appreciation began, which suggests that exchange rates are not the only factor in this industry's predicament. However, it is still useful to consider the overall effects of exchange rates on this sector. One recent study has evaluated the effects of movements in the real exchange rates on employment and output in U.S. manufacturing industries in the 1970s and 1980s (Branson 1986). Although this study does not directly estimate the effects of trade on employment, it does provide information about the relative trade-sensitivity of the motor vehicle industry employment.

Between 1977 and 1980, the period of rapid import growth, the value of the dollar was falling. Branson's results indicate that exchange rate effects tended to *increase* employment during this period (despite the fact the overall employment in this industry was declining in this period). Between 1980 and the first quarter of 1985, the value of the dollar (as measured in Branson's study) increased by 54.6%. His study suggests that employment fell by 25.7% in the motor vehicle industry and by 9.0% in the manufacturing sector as a whole because of exchange rate effects. However, actual employment in the auto industry rose by 11.5% over this period. The tendency of exchange rates to depress employment in this period was outweighed by increases in aggregate demand, by the fall in the real price of energy and by trade restrictions which all tended to increase overall employment in the auto industry.

Two conclusions about trade and the auto industry emerge from analysis of Branson's results. First, changes in the value of the dollar were not responsible for the dramatic rise in imports which took place over the 1977-1980 period. Second, the auto industry is much more sensitive to exchange rate effects than the average manufacturing industry, which reinforces the argument that relative manufacturing costs play a large role in the competitive problems of the domestic auto industry.

    e. Summary. Three conclusions emerge from this review:

1.   There would have been 115,000 more direct job opportunities in the vehicle industry in 1978 if trade had been balanced, and 125,000 more in 1980 (an 8.7% increase in 2 years).

2.   Vehicle trade has a much larger effect on labor demand in supplier industries than in the industry itself. In 1978 the total (direct + indirect) labor content of vehicle trade was 347,000 work-years, or 39% of the labor content of all

U.S. trade in that year. By 1985 the total reached 661,000 work years, despite the effects of trade protection.

3.　In the 1970s trade appears to have been the most important factor in the decline of auto sector employment. Lawrence finds that between 1970 and 1980 the growth in net imports had a labor content equal to 11.1% of industry employment in 1970. Constant share analysis suggests that even when comparing the boom year of 1973 with the 1980 recession, trade and domestic demand contributed almost equally to the decrease in employment. Changes in the value of the dollar did not play an important role in the industry's decline in this period.

2. The Effects of Trade Protection: 1980-84

Between 1977 and 1980, the Japanese share of the number of cars sold in the U.S. auto market nearly doubled, rising from 11.9% to 22.4%. In 1980, Japanese firms planned to increase motor vehicle assembly capacity by an additional 20% through 1983 (U.S. Dept. of Transportation 1981), enough capacity to double their share of the U.S. market again in the early 1980s. From 1978 to 1980, the growing recession reduced the total number of autos sold in the U.S. by 23%. In the same period the number of Japanese imports sold **rose** by 28%, leading to a 30% decline in domestic production. 238,000 auto industry workers were on temporary or indefinite layoff in December, 1980 (U.S. Department of Transportation, 1982). The threat of further extensive job loss in the auto industry led to congressional hearings on a series of protectionist measures (i.e. local content legislation) and resulted in an agreement between the U.S. and Japanese governments to "voluntarily" restrain the number of Japanese autos exported to the U.S.[30] Protection of the domestic truck market was also increased substantially in 1980 through an administrative measure which increased the tariff on Japanese truck imports from 4% to 25%.[31]

From the U.S. perspective there were at least two reasons for supporting the Japanese export quotas. First there was the potential for further job loss. Second, there was a widely expressed desire to give the industry some "breathing space" to allow it to eliminate or reduce the MCD and to catch up to Japanese innovations in auto production technology. As shown above, by 1980 Japanese producers had lower wages, higher rates of labor productivity, and lower parts costs than their U.S. competitors. If the U.S. auto makers were to become competitive in small cars they would have to respond to problems in each of these areas.

Preserving employment and improving competitiveness would appear on the surface to be conflicting goals. However, they are in fact closely linked, for several reasons. First, unless the competitiveness of the domestic industry is improved, there will be very large losses in domestic market share in the future. Thus, the choice for domestic workers is not whether to maintain current employment levels or accept productivity improvements which reduce the labor content of autos. The choice is to either make those productivity improvements or lose a much larger share of employment to imported products. This argument is reinforced by the fact that 2 workers are displaced in supplier industries for each worker displaced in the auto industry, as discussed above. Thus it is in the interest of both labor and management to improve productivity and product quality in the domestic auto industry.

This section will examine the trends and determinants of employment by and the competitiveness of U.S. auto makers over the period of the VRAs. The effects of the breathing space were apparently negated from the outset by the failure of the U.S. government to develop policies which were appropriate for the problems and the structure of this particular industry. The domestic motor vehicle industry is highly concentrated and most of the workforce is represented by a powerful labor union, the United Auto Workers (UAW). Given the structure of the industry and its labor market, a *quid pro quo* that would restrain the growth of wages and prices in exchange for protection could have helped the industry use the VRA period to increase its competitiveness. There would be at least three essential ingredients in such an agreement. The first would provide incentives for (or require) the firms in the industry to limit prices and profits. The second would involve new co-operative labor-management efforts to reorganize production to increase productivity and product quality through continued capital investments, use of new technology and new patterns of job responsibilities. The third would involve commitments to restrain wage growth and address the high cost of white-collar labor in the industry. Union participation in reorganization plans would be an essential part of any quid pro quo agreement.

Without an external restraint, firms in such a highly concentrated industry would be unable to resist the opportunity to raise prices and profits under import protection, leading workers to demand their fair share of the pie in the form of wage increases.[32] An effort was apparently made in 1980 and 1981 to reach an agreement, linked to the VRAs, between the industry and the UAW which would be enforced by the U.S. Government. At least some members of both the industry and the union expressed the desire for a three-way pact but the government refused to participate, opting instead to negotiate the VRA with the Japanese government and 'allow market forces' to handle the adjustment processes.[33] This section will review prior research which suggests that the administration's failure to take advantage of this opportunity led to dramatic increases in the prices of all automobiles sold in the U.S. and may have damaged the long-run competitiveness of the domestic auto industry.

3. The Effects of the VRAs on Quality, Output and Employment Patterns

An assessment of the employment effects of the VRAs depends on an assessment of the potential market share of Japanese imports in the early 1980s without the restrictions. A number of recent reports from academic economists and Government agencies which have addressed this issue are analyzed below. The MCD is a critical factor in the debate over the potential share of Japanese imports in U.S. auto sales. The Japanese advantage was concentrated in the small car market segment (compact and subcompact vehicle classes) when the VRAs went into effect. The small car share of the numbers of units sold of the U.S. auto market rose steadily from 30.8% in the 1970-73 period to a peak of 55.8% in 1979-81, as a result of the rapid growth of energy prices in the 1970s (section B, above). The decline of gas prices in the early 1980s reduced the small car share to about 50%.

a. Quality Upgrading and the VRAs. In 1980 87.7% of Japanese imports (in terms of the number of units sold) were concentrated in the small car class (66.6% subcompacts and 20.9% compacts).[34] Luxury small cars and sports cars, the remaining segment, represented 12.3% of Japanese exports in 1980. By 1984, under the effects of the VRAs the share of compacts had risen to 33.4% and the luxury/sports share to 18.2% of Japanese exports to the U.S. These trends illustrate the shift to higher priced models that has been one result of the VRAs.

Robert Feenstra (1985a, 1985b) has studied the price and quality-change effects of the VRAs. The basic intuition behind Feenstra's work is straightforward. Faced with a numerical quota on the number of cars that can be sold in the U.S. market a Japanese producer will maximize profits by selling cars with the highest per-unit profit, which are generally the more expensive cars. Feenstra has carefully broken down the effects of the quota into pure price change, and the effects of quality upgrading. He finds that "nearly all of the rise in [suggested retail] import prices can be explained by the upgrading of individual models (Feenstra, 1985a, p 56)." He found that for a sample of Japanese cars average unit value rose by 29.4% between 1981 and 1985, while the average quality level rose by 21.7%.[35] For a sample of U.S.-made small cars average prices rose by only 14.6% and quality by only 9.1% over the same period (Feenstra, 1985a). The VRAs caused Japanese producers to build more expensive, more "heavily loaded" cars for the U.S. market.

b. Tariffs vs. Quotas. The shift to higher valued exports is one reason why a tariff on Japanese imports would have been a more effective policy measure than a quota. A tariff would not have created the incentive for Japanese producers to move into more highly valued models, as Feenstra (1985b) showed in an analysis of the truck tariff increase. The quality of Japanese truck exports increased by only 11.5% between 1981 and 1985, and most of that growth occurred in 1985, in response to new model offerings in the U.S. There are at least two reasons why a tariff might have been preferable to a quota for domestic producers in the automobile industry. First, the quota gave the Japanese production experience in larger, more profitable models. It also created incentives, discussed below, which led them to sell technology to Korean producers to help them penetrate the low-priced end of the U.S. auto market. These acts gave foreign producers learning curve experience which may have permanently improved their competitiveness in these market segments. The quota also transferred substantial profits to Japanese producers that would have been retained by the U.S. Government under a tariff.

c. The Output Effects of the VRAs. The actual market shares of Japanese producers and of all imports from 1979 to 1987 are shown in Tables 1 and 2, above. A number of recent reports have estimated the potential Japanese market share in the absence of the VRAs. Three of the most widely quoted studies will now be discussed, to establish the general methodological approach in the literature. The principal problem with the published literature is that it fails to adequately consider the dynamic supply-side behavior of Japanese producers and the effects of the oligopoly structure of the U.S. vehicle industry, and thus fails to adequately explain the effects of the VRAs on output, prices and employment in the U.S. auto market.

Crandall (1984) simply asserts, with no justification, that "It is difficult to see how the [VRAs] could have shifted more than 8 percentage points of the market from Japanese imports to U.S. cars by 1983." The USITC (1985a) fitted a logarithmic time trend to the Japanese share of the U.S. auto market for 1967-80. Although this estimation "predicted share values that were lower than actual values [in the late 1970s]" it was used anyway to project market shares of Japanese producers for the period 1981-84. The USITC estimated that in 1984 Japanese producers would have gained a 28.4% share of the U.S. market without the VRAs.

A logarithmic time-trend underestimates the effect of the VRAs on Japanese market share because it does not reflect the capacity expansion plans and dynamic market growth strategies of the Japanese firms. Crandall's estimate and the USITC's time trend analysis of Japanese market shares fail to account for the dramatic increase in the Japanese market share that occurred between 1979 and 1980 (Table 1), when the Japanese share of total vehicle sales in the U.S. jumped 8 percentage points in a single year, to a total of 22.2% of U.S. vehicle market. A risk averse member of the UAW might reasonably have wondered if the Japanese were going to gain 4 to 5 percentage points a year for the next several years. At that point Japanese producers had built an effective marketing network, they had a quality product that met the needs of half of the U.S. auto market, and they had developed a substantial cost advantage. In 1980, the U.S. industry's chances of preventing rapid growth in Japan's market share were probably quite small.

d. The Price Effects of the VRAs. The USITC, and other authors, also overlook the signs of a substantial decline in the competitiveness of the U.S. auto industry in the late 1970s. The studies reviewed in section B, above, suggest that Japanese producers had developed a substantial competitive advantage in small cars by 1980, one that would grow with the value of the dollar in the early 1980s. The pricing policies of the U.S. auto makers only served to make matters worse. This problem is illustrated by Feenstra's (1984a) analysis of the effects of the VRAs on employment, quality and prices in the U.S. auto market. Between 1980 and 1981 Feenstra found that the prices of Japanese autos rose about 8.4%. Two-thirds of this amount (5.3%) is attributed to quality change and one-third (3.1%) to pure price change. He maintains that the effects of the quotas on U.S. output and employment can be estimated by evaluating the effect of the 3.1% of pure price change on production and revenues of U.S. producers, using a range of estimates of the elasticity of demand for imported autos.[36] He finds that, depending on the elasticity used, the employment-content of excluded Japanese autos ranged between 5,600 and 22,300 workers in 1981.

The critical flaw in Feenstra's analysis is that he ignored the fact (revealed in his own data) that the real prices of U.S. small cars rose by 11.1% in 1980 and 6% in 1981, and that without the VRA effect on Japanese prices, there would have been very large shifts in market share to Japanese cars in the long run from these domestic price increases. It is estimated that the cross-price elasticity of demand between U.S. cars and Japanese imports (in the long run) is estimated to lie somewhere between 2 and 5 (Toder 1978). Thus a 15% increase in the relative price of U.S. small cars (if maintained) would sift 30% to 75% of demand to Japanese producers in the long run. The domestic market was not in equilibrium in 1981 when the VRAs were enacted. Toder's elasticity estimates suggest that the employment effects could have been orders of magnitude larger than Feenstra's estimates by the mid-1980s.

The prices of domestic cars would probably not have increased so dramatically in 1980 and 1981, relative to competing imported products, if there were more domestic producers and if trade protection had not been anticipated by domestic producers in 1980. None of the models discussed so far have explicitly considered the effects of market structure on performance in this market during the 1980s, thus ignoring one of the most important determinants of the behavior of domestic producers under trade protection.

There is one paper in the literature on the VRAs which does explicitly consider the effects of oligopoly power in modeling the problem. Gomez-Ibanez, Leone and O'Connell (1983) use a simulation model to estimate the affects of quotas on auto imports. Their model assumes that Japanese producers maximize profits by employing Stackleberg-leader behavior (with U.S. firms as passive reactors). This simulation yields estimated employment effects of the same magnitude as Crandall and the USITC. Gomez-Ibanez, *et al*, do not attempt to justify the particular oligopoly solution chosen. Although the VRAs did effectively cartelize the Japanese producers, it does not seem reasonable to view the 3 major producers in the U.S., who collectively control over two-thirds of the domestic auto market, as passive reactors in this market.

e. Summary. All of the studies reviewed in this section, with the exception of Gomez-Ibanez, Leone and O'Connell (1983), ignored the role of oligopoly behavior in assessing the effects of the VRAs on trade and employment patterns in the U.S. auto industry. Each of these studies also considered only the direct effects of the VRAs on U.S. employment, thus inherently overlooking the effects of changes in auto output on the demand for other manufactured products and services in the domestic economy, thus ignoring the employment effects of the VRAs on other sectors.

In order to develop a better understanding of the influence of market structure on the competitiveness of the auto industry and on the performance of this sector under the VRAs, a new empirical model of the U.S. auto market during the 1971-1986 period will be developed, estimated and interpreted in the remainder of this study.

NOTES

5. See Altshuler, *et al* (1984), Chapter 2, pp. 11-46.

6. This figure includes the U.S. Census Bureau's Standard Industrial Classification (SIC categories 371, motor vehicles and parts, and 3465, automotive stampings. Note that the number of units produced in the U.S. also reached an historic high in 1978.

7. Seventy-four percent of auto stampings (SIC 3465) were produced in Michigan, Indiana and Ohio. 62% of parts production (SIC 3714) took place in Michigan, Ohio, New York and Indiana (U.S. Department of Labor 1985c).

8. Kwoka provides evidence to support this hypothesis for 1978, when the dollar fell by 30% against the Yen. U.S. producers raised small car prices rather than holding them down and expanding market share during this period. He also provides data which indicates that even when the domestic industry did have a cost advantage in the early 1960s, profit maximizing behavior also led it to accommodate an increase in import sales in the U.S., although it did use frequent changes in model characteristics to limit import growth during that period.

5. See, for example, Altshuler, *et al,* (1984) and Cole and Yakushiji (1984).

6. Note that average sales over the 1979-1986 business cycle were diminished by the long, steep recession of the early 1980s. U.S. trade protection substantially increased average vehicle prices in the early 1980s, thus reducing vehicle demand (relative to other goods). The U.S. International Trade Commission estimated that the VRAs reduced total auto demand by about three percent in 1984 (USITC 1985a).

11. The small car shares discussed here are approximations which sum the compact and subcompact shares of U.S. producers *(Automotive News)* and the Japanese import share (USITC 1985c). This excludes imports of European small cars. However, the European share of the U.S. auto market is less than 1%.

12. The data for Apparent Domestic Consumption and Net Trade in this table are measures of the value of final sales, from *Citibase*. The data for the value of imports are measures of the wholesale cost of

imports at the port of entry, from international trade statistics. Thus the import data are based on lower unit prices than the data on the value of final sales (reflecting the difference between wholesale and retail prices). Thus the import data in this table under estimate the value of imported vehicles at the point of final sale in the U.S. The data for the wholesale values of apparent domestic consumption were not available from published sources for the period shown in this table.

13. Nominal trade values were converted to constant 1982 dollars using Gross National Product implicit price deflators for the U.S.

14. The Auto Products Trade Act (APTA) of 1965 eliminated tariffs subject to certain performance requirements in new motor vehicles and parts between the U.S. and Canada (USITC 1985b). This agreement applies to almost all trade in new vehicles between the two countries.

15. Aizcorbe, *et at,* estimate that the MCD was $2,369 in 1980 and $1,309 in 1982. They are careful to note that their study was estimating *marginal* cost differentials, whereas the engineering studies refer to *average* cost differentials and hence the estimates are not directly comparable.

16. These estimates are based on a study by Abernathy, Harbour and Henn (1981), which originally estimated a landed cost differential of $1,650. Flynn revised their estimates to correct a problem in the way in which adjustments were made to account for differences in model mixes and levels of vertical integration of U.S. and Japanese firms.

17. Includes the effects of both wage rate and labor productivity differences.

18. Includes only transportation to port of entry. U.S. delivery costs excluded.

19. The studies reviewed by Cole and Yakushiji, and by Flynn display a wide variation in assumptions about labor inputs, ranging from 38.6 to 99 hours per vehicle produced in Japan (mean estimate of 64.4 hours), ranging from 59.9 to 144 hours per vehicle produced in the U.S. (mean estimate of 108.2 hours). These estimates are for labor used directly by major producers, adjusted to correct for differences in model mix and levels of vertical integration. Wage rate estimates display a

smaller variance, with mean estimated wages of $10.43 per hour in Japan and $19.47 per hour in the U.S. (Flynn 1982, p. 53).

20. Some studies assigned joint effects to wages and some to productivity, although they are a combined result of both factors.

21. Wages for 1987 were estimated using 1980-83 home currency growth rates. Japanese wage rates, measured in Yen, grew slightly faster than those in the U.S. in this period. This reflects the strong seniority premia in the Japanese wage system.

22. See Kwoka (1984) for data on advertising costs per unit sold for different manufacturers.

23. This calculation assumes that the MCD is accurately measured in Table 3. There is substantial uncertainty about the actual size of the MCD, and how it has changed in recent years, as discussed above with respect to the work of Aizcorbe, *et at* (1987). That discussion argues that the MCD in the early 1980s would be eliminated at an exchange rate somewhere between 151.9 and 105.4 yen per dollar.

24. See "Strong yen spurs parts imports from NICs, China", *Japan Economic Journal,* October 11, 1986, p.11.

25. Note, however, that the VRAs were substantially relaxed, effective April 1, 1986, increasing from a limit of 1,850,000 cars in Japanese fiscal year 1985 to 2,300,000 in 1986 (Wards Communications, Inc. 1988).

26. The job opportunity figures discussed here must be interpreted carefully. Strictly speaking, these figures represent the labor content of trade in the given years. If the trade deficit were eliminated (e.g., by import quotas) domestic job opportunities would rise by these amounts only if domestic products were substituted for imports at the same price and in the same quantities, and if there were no simultaneous changes in other factors such as the level of aggregate demand.

27. The figures here are an approximation derived from the data in U.S. Dept. of Labor 1985b, which used the 1977 input-output table and 1984 employment/output relationships to estimate direct and indirect employment required for each $1 million dollar of sales to final users of motor vehicles. For each work-year of direct labor input 2.02 work

years of indirect labor inputs were required in 1977, according to this
input-output table. The ratio of direct to indirect employment (based on
1977 input-output coefficients) will vary only if *relative* wage rates
change over time. Between 1978 and 1984 average weekly earnings
grew by 50.1% for all manufacturing jobs and by 51.3% for the motor
vehicle industry. Thus the ratio calculated using 1984
employment/output relationships will closely approximate the ratio for
1978.

28. Lawrence uses a constant share analysis to evaluate the effects of
trade over the 1978-82 period. However, in 1982 the VRAs were
already in effect, restraining Japanese auto exports to the U.S., reducing
the actual effects of trade in the 1978-82 period.

29. The most important reason for the difference between the constant
share and Lawrence estimates is that the constant share approach
corrects for differences in aggregate demand by calculating the
employment content of auto trade in 1980, if import market shares had
remained at their 1973 levels (instead of using actual trade-related
employment in 1973 for comparisons, as Lawrence does). The constant
share approach thus uses a lower estimate of base year (1973)
employment than does Lawrence, and the *change* in trade related
employment between 1973 and 1980 is therefore larger with the
constant share approach. The estimate of the actual employment content
of trade in 1980 is the same with both techniques.

30. Conditions in the auto industry in 1980 lead to increasing pressure
for protection from Japanese auto exports. In June, 1980 the Ford Motor
Co. and the United Auto Workers filed a joint petition for relief under
section 201 of the Trade Act of 1974. The U.S. International Trade
Commission denied the petition in November of 1980. In early 1981
legislation to restrict imports of Japanese cars was gaining support in
Congress. On May 1, 1981 MITI announced a Voluntary Restraint
Agreement (VRA) that would reduce the number of autos exports to the
U.S. to 1,832,500, 7% less than in 1980, for the Japanese fiscal year
which began April 1, 1981. The VRA continued for 2 more years at a
constant level of exports and was extended for a fourth year at
2,015,000 units, a 10% increase (USITC, 1985a). The VRA expired on
April 1, 1985 but the Japanese government extended it for 1985-86, at
a level of 2.3 million units per year, 24.3% more than were allowed in
1984-85 ("Rise in Car Exports Confirmed by Japan", *The New York
Times, March 29, 1985*). The Export Restraint was renewed at the 2.3

million unit level in 1986-87 *(The New York Times, February 13, 1986),* despite the opposition of the U.S. government. The restraints were maintained by the Japanese government at the 2.3 million unit level through the 1989-1990 period. However, as a result of the rise in the Yen, Japanese auto exports to the U.S. failed to reach this level in 1988.

31. Feenstra provides an interesting history of the small truck tariff: "During the 1970s Japan exported an increasing number of compact trucks to the U.S., most as cab/chassis with some final assembly needed. In 1980 Congress asked the USITC to study the possible reclassification of Japanese imports, from "parts of trucks" as then applied to "complete or unfinished trucks." The former carried a tariff rate of 4%, whereas the latter had a duty of 25%. This unusually high rate was a result of the "chicken war" between the United States in Europe in 1962-63, when the U.S. retaliated against higher tariffs on poultry sales to West Germany. In 1980 the U.S. Customs Service announced that effective August 21 imported lightweight cab/chassis would be reclassified as complete trucks (Feenstra, 1985, pp.12-13)".

32. Firms and workers in any industry given trade protection could be expected to behave in a similar fashion in the short-run. However, the motor vehicle industry has a history of above average rates of return on equity and a high degree of concentration (Kwoka, 1984), and wages well above the manufacturing average, suggesting the existence of substantial barriers to entry. The temporary effects of trade policy on wages, price and profits could be expected to persist in an oligopoly with such market power.

33. Private interviews with senior auto executives by John Zysman and Laura Tyson, principal investigators with the Berkeley Roundtable on International Economy.

34. Market segment data in this paragraph from USITC 1985a.

35. (Feenstra 1985b). Quality is defined by fundamental auto characteristics such as size, power, type of transmission and the inclusion of power steering and air conditioning. Feenstra estimated the value of these attributes using a hedonic pricing model.

36. Feenstra claims that the portion of the price effect which can be attributed to quality change did not decrease demand for autos, since these were real services which consumers were willing to pay for. Given the 3.1% residual price effect, and price elasticity estimates ranging from 2 to 5, he calculated the effects on revenue, production and employment using per/unit revenue and employment coefficients from unspecified sources.

CHAPTER III
THE MODEL

This chapter will derive and specify the theoretical model used to analyze demand patterns and the interaction between trade policy and market concentration in the U.S. auto industry. The chapter begins with a review of conceptual approaches used to model oligopolistic interactions at the industry level. A simplified model incorporating the effects of oligopoly behavior is identified and used as the basis for the model which is then developed for this study.

Modern oligopoly theory has produced many different models of market structure and firm interaction. A principle challenge for any empirical study of industry conduct and performance is to identify that particular form of oligopoly interaction that best characterizes a given sector. Beginning with a seminal paper by Iwata (1974) a large literature has developed that attempts to empirically estimate oligopoly conduct for a variety of industries.[1]

The measurement of oligopoly interaction is complicated by extensive product differentiation. Gelfand and Spiller (1985) estimate a model for an industry with two products. However, with even two products the number of cross-elasticity and interaction terms grows quite large. With an industry as complex as automobiles, with several hundred distinct product varieties, direct estimation of conduct parameters becomes impossible.[2] It is also important to note that when product differentiation is treated as a strategic variable, the number of possible forms of oligopoly behavior that can sustain positive monopoly rents grows. The ability to sustain positive profits does not depend on whether firms choose prices or quantities as strategic variables, as is the case with Bertrand (Nash) models of homogeneous product industries.[3]

A. The Baker and Bresnahan Model[4]

Baker and Bresnahan (1985a and 1985b) developed an econometric model for measuring the market power of firms in differentiated product industries, without estimating all of the possible cross elasticities of demand between competing products. The model developed here is derived from the Baker and Bresnahan model. Baker and Bresnahan have developed a new econometric approach which makes it possible to identify and estimate the residual demand curve facing a firm in an oligopoly with differentiated products. The basic concept involves use of the average revenue received by the firm for all units of a similar product that it sells in a given time period. This allows specification of a single demand curve for all of the firm's products.

Baker and Bresnahan's differentiated oligopoly model is theoretically distinct from Chamberlinian models of monopolistic competition, although the basic graphic interpretations are similar.[5] The residual demand curve estimated by Baker and Bresnahan takes into account the expected output reactions of all other firms in the industry to a change in the firm's own price or quantity. A change in the firm's own price can be interpreted as a proportional change in the prices of all of its products.

Baker and Bresnahan test a number of hypotheses about oligopoly behavior. If a firm's own output (Q_1 in equation 1, below) has no effect on the price it receives, then its residual demand curve will have no slope, i.e. the firm has no market power. They also show that in an industry where product differentiation is the only source of market power, the residual demand elasticity will be directly related to the firm's markup of price over marginal cost. Finally, Baker and Bresnahan test for collusion in a differentiated product industry by comparing the residual demand elasticity for a given firm with demand elasticity for the industry as a whole. Their basic model will be described next, and their model will be modified for use in this study of the auto industry.

Let the (inverse) demand curve for an individual firm in the industry be:

(1) $$P_1 = h_1(Q_1, \underset{\sim}{Q}, Y; \alpha_1)$$

where P_1 and Q_1 are firm 1's average revenue per unit and total quantity of output, $\underset{\sim}{Q}$ is a vector of other firms' products, Y is a vector of exogenous macroeconomic variables that affect demand, and α_1 is a vector of parameters for the system.

The demand curves for the remaining (n-1) firms in this industry can be summarized, using $\underset{\sim}{P}$ to represent a vector of equations, as:

(2) $$P = h(Q,Q_1,Y;\alpha).$$

The solution to each firm's first order condition is specified in the usual MR = MC form, with explicit acknowledgement of each firm's (consistent) conjectural variations about the behavior of all other firms:

(3) $$MC(Q_i,\ W,\ W_i;\ \beta_i) = MR(Q, Q_i, Y, \alpha_i;\ \Theta_i)$$

$$= P + g(Q, Q_i, Y, \alpha_i;\ \Theta_i)\ Q$$

In this formulation, MC depends on firm output, Q_i; a vector of industry-wide factor prices, W; and on a set of firm-specific cost factors, W_i, that are not included in the industry-wide vector W, for example firm specific production capacity (which will influence the slope and location of the firm's MC curve in the short-run). The β_i represent firm-specific cost-function parameters. MR depends on the demand parameters from equation 2, and on a measure of firm interaction, Θ_i. While the conjectural variations models discussed above all estimate the α_i, β_i, and Θ_i, separately, Baker and Bresnahan's principle theoretical innovation is to "estimate only their joint impact on market power through the slope of the residual demand curve (Baker and Bresnahan, 1985b, p. 8)".

Baker and Bresnahan then factor Q out of equation (1), by solving simultaneously the system of equations (2) and (3), above. Residual demand curves for individual firms are then estimated. At this point, the model developed here diverges from the Baker and Bresnahan model in two specific ways: Price (Bertrand) competition is assumed and a reduced form model including separate equations for P_i and Q_i is estimated, instead of using a two- or three- stage least squares approach to estimate the complete residual demand curve system.

B. A Residual Demand Model for the U.S. Auto industry

It is assumed that automakers set prices, for each of three size classes of cars, once each model year and then allow quantities to adjust to clear the market. Firm-specific demand (U.S. sales of a given size class, in a given period, Q_i^6) depends on the firm's own price (P_i), the prices of its competitors (P_j), a vector of macroeconomic and structural variables (Y), and on the costs of production for its competitors (which will affect the quantities supplied by other producers):

(4) $Q_i = f(P_i, P_j, Y, W, W_l)$,

where W is a vector of industry wide factor costs and W_l is a vector of firm-specific factor costs for firms other than firm i. The estimated parameters of firm i's residual demand curve will reflect the reactions of other firms in the industry to changes in firm i's price level.

Each firm is assumed to set output by equating marginal cost with marginal revenue:

(5) $MC_i(Q_i, W, W_i) = Q_i + P_i g(P_i, P_j, W, W_l)$,

where W_i is a vector of firm specific factor costs for firm i and g is the partial derivative of equation 4 with respect to own price. Equilibrium price and output levels for firm i are determined jointly by these two equations. This specification clearly establishes that the parameters of the demand equation will be identified when there exist firm-specific cost variables W_i.

The most fundamental econometric problem posed by the system of equations 4 and 5 is that the parameters of firm i's supply function cannot be identified because every variable which affects residual demand will also appear in the supply equation, through the marginal revenue equation.[7] Without estimates of supply behavior, it is impossible to use equations 4 and 5 to estimate the effects of the VRAs on output and prices in the domestic auto industry.

1. A Reduced Form Model

An alternative to estimating the full system of demand and supply equations is to estimate a reduced form model. Equation (4) and a supply relationship for firm 1, analogous to equation (5), are solved simultaneously to derive separate expressions for P_i and Q_i. A model of the following general form was estimated for each of 3 size-classes of cars (small, medium and large) for the four U.S.-based auto assemblers, General Motors, Ford, Chrysler and American Motors(AM):[8]

(6) $$Q_i = m(P_j, Y, W, W_l, W_i),$$

(7) $$P_i = n(P_j, Y, W, W_l, W_i).$$

The actual variables included in the vectors P_j, Y, W, W_l and W_i will be discussed in Chapter V, below.

A reduced form model does not directly estimate residual demand elasticities, in contrast to Baker and Bresnahan's (1985) model. However, it will provide estimates of the ways in which the domestic industry *responded* to the imposition of the quotas, as reflected in the effects of the quotas on output and prices in each firm/size class included in the study. Equations 6 and 7 thus form a model of outcomes or performance in the domestic industry which is determined, in part, by residual demand elasticities. Conduct and structural parameters are imbedded in the reduced form coefficients and cannot be directly evaluated using this technique.

In simplest terms, when market protection is awarded to a firm with market power, it will be perceived as an outward shift in its residual demand curve. A firm faced with such a demand curve shift can choose to increase price, quantity sold, or both. A firm's choice of price and quantity will depend on its market power and on the reactions of other firms to changes in its own price or output levels (as reflected in the residual demand elasticity facing that firm in the market).[9] The model estimated in Chapter V will reveal the degree to which the VRAs affected both prices and output levels of domestic auto producers. It is entirely possible that the market power of one or more domestic producers was so enhanced by the VRAs that they caused a reduction in firm output, relative to levels that would have been achieved without protection.[10]

The model developed in equations 6 and 7 will also be applied to the market for imports. Factor markets are also assumed to have been affected by the VRAs, which will in turn have an impact on the product markets, reflected in equations 6 and 7.

2. *Import Markets*

A reduced form model, analogous to equations 6 and 7 above, will be estimated for imported cars. All imports are aggregated together in this estimation to simplify the analysis. This approach treats imports as the competitive fringe in the domestic auto market. No single brand of imports achieved a market share of greater than 7% of the U.S. market in the period covered by this study[11]. It is possible to view the VRAs as having the effect of cartelizing the Japanese auto industry. However, even taken as a block, the Japanese have never had more than a 24% share of the number of cars sold in the U.S. (USITC 1985c), much smaller than GM's average share of 45% in the 1970s and 43.7% in the 1980s. Thus, even when viewed as a cartel, Japanese producers were still not the most dominant players in the domestic industry. One advantage of including aggregate import equations is that they complete the picture of the domestic auto market, allowing for analysis of the total effects of the quotas on prices, output and the number of cars sold, by domestic- and foreign-based producers.[12]

3. Factor Costs

If the labor market in the auto industry is sufficiently concentrated on either the supply or the demand sides, then wages will not competitively determined. A situation in which there is significant concentration on both sides of the market can be viewed as a bilateral monopoly or oligopoly. Theoretical research on labor market structures has shown that wages will be determined by negotiations between the parties in question under conditions of involving bilateral market power. In cases where product markets are also concentrated, such negotiations can result in labor's capture of a share of the monopoly profits earned in the product market.

Alternatively, if labor supply curves are upward sloping a VRA-induced increase in labor demand in the domestic market would also put upward pressure on wages under a purely competitive labor market structure. In both cases a VRA-related increase in wages would have an impact on firm-specific marginal costs, and hence on output and prices. Thus wages and other factor costs are treated as endogenous variables in this model.

VRA-related changes in factor costs are a secondary channel through which these policies can effect domestic output and prices. If the VRAs resulted in higher wages, then in a competitive product market these wage effects would offset some of the (positive) effects of the VRAs on output and reinforce their (positive) effects on prices. This model will provide empirical evidence on the nature of these secondary effects in this highly concentrated industry.

The cost of capital, on a firm-specific basis, includes profit as reported annually to the SEC. Profits may be influenced by any factors which change the output, price, or price-cost markup of the firm. Thus profits, and hence firm-specific capital costs, may also have been affected by the VRAs.

In principle wages and profits could be influenced by any of the variables which effect own output and price in equations 6 and 7 above. However, price variables were omitted from the factor cost equations in order to avoid problems with non-linearities in model simulation. Factor cost equations were estimated for three groups of variables: 1) the total hourly, unionized labor cost for all three "big three" assembly firms in the U.S., under United Auto Worker labor contracts (a component of the Vector W); 2) the firm-specific cost of all labor, including union, non-union and management workers (both domestic and foreign) for GM, Ford and Chrysler (a component of W_i); and 3) the firm-specific cost of capital for the same firms (another component of W_i).[13] The same basic model was used to estimate all of these factor cost (FC) equations:

$$(8) \qquad\qquad FC_i = k(Y, W).$$

The variables included in the vectors Y and W are discussed in Chapter V.

The model developed here will be estimated in Chapter V and the results will be used in chapter VI to simulate output and prices in the domestic industry under alternative scenarios, and to estimate the impact of the VRAs on industry wage and profit levels.[14] Chapter IV will present and discuss the data used to estimate this model.

NOTES

1. These studies generally attempt to measure each firm's conjectural variation about the response of other firms in the industry to a change in its own output or price. Examples include Applebaum (1979 and 1982), Gollop and Roberts (1979), Just and Chern (1980), Spiller and Favaro (1984), Sullivan (1985), and Summner (1981). Bresnahan (1981b) presents a useful theoretical introduction and overview of the theoretical and econometric concepts underlying attempts to estimate market power. Hwang (1984) extends the theoretical model to questions of international trade.

2. Bresnahan (1981a) estimates a model that tests several different oligopoly solution concepts to explain auto industry conduct, but does not directly estimate conjectural variation parameters.

3. For a simple example of positive oligopoly profits with product differentiation and Bertrand (price) competition see Friedman (1977), chapter 3. Note that while the ability to sustain positive rents in a differentiated product oligopoly does not depend on whether prices or quantities are chosen as strategic variables, the *levels* of prices, quantities and profits obtained in the market do depend on the choice of strategic variable.

4. This section of the paper paraphrases the presentation of the model developed by Baker and Bresnahan to estimate the elasticity of demand facing a single firm in the U.S. brewing industry (Baker and Bresnahan, 1985a and 1985b). I have used their notation and variable descriptions, with minor modifications for clarity of presentation.

5. This point is clarified in footnote 6 of Baker and Bresnahan (1985a).

6. The (quarterly) quantity data in this model were seasonally adjusted for GM, Ford and Chrysler, to avoid having to include seasonal dummy variables in the model. The quantity data for AM could not be seasonally adjusted, because there were periods in which AM had no sales in each of these size classes.

7. There is also a major practical barrier to estimating the residual *demand* curve equations. In order to obtain reasonable estimates of the parameters of the demand curve, the excluded variables in the supply equation (W_i) must have a significant impact on the position of the

supply curve. If the effects of factor costs are small, relative to the demand shift parameters in the MR equation, it will be difficult to obtain reliable estimates of demand parameters. The importance of marginal revenue in the supply equation will rise with the degree of concentration and market power in any given industry.

8. Large cars were not sold in the U.S. by AM during the period of the quotas, so these equations are estimated only for small and medium AM cars.

9. Baker and Bresnahan have shown that the residual elasticity of demand facing an individual firm "depends on both structural demand function elasticities...and reaction function elasticities (Baker and Bresnahan, 1985, p.432".

10. The level of output can fall if protection increases a firm's market power. If demand is linear, an increase in market power would be reflected in an increase in the *slope* of a firm's residual demand curve.

11. Toyota achieved a share of 6.85% of U.S. auto sales in 1982, the highest share ever achieved by a Japanese auto maker in this market (USITC, 1985c).

12. Note that imports from Canada are not considered separately from domestically produced autos in this model. Model-level sales data by country of origin are not available for domestic producers, on a quarterly basis.

Note also that domestic production of cars in U.S. facilities owned by foreign-based producers is not explicitly modeled here. Transplant production is considered in Chapter VI.

13. Labor and Capital cost figures were not reported for the later years of this study for American Motors Corporation, after a controlling interest in AMC was acquired by the French firm Regie Nationale des Usines Renault in 1980 *(The Wall Street Journal*, December 17, 1980, p.6). Therefore AM factor costs do not appear in any of the regression equations, nor were they separately estimated under the factor cost models.

14. Alternatively, the estimated factor cost values derived from equation 8 could have been used as instruments in equations 3 and 4, above, and then used in the simulations in the ways described here. However,

because of the large number of variables included when actually estimating equations 3 and 4, and the high adjusted R^2 of the labor cost equations (.87 to .98) the costs of using instruments for factor costs would probably exceed any gain in the efficiency or accuracy of the estimates.

CHAPTER IV
DATA GENERATION AND HISTORICAL ANALYSIS

The first three sections of this chapter will discuss the data collected and variables generated for this study. Section D will summarize and interpret some of the more interesting historical data assembled here. The model specified in chapter III requires three data sets, one for macroeconomic variables, one for auto prices and output levels and one for factor costs. The three sets of variables included consist of:

(1) Macroeconomic variables:
> Implicit price deflators
> Gross National Product
> Gasoline prices
> Interest rates
> Time trend and structural dummy variables;

(2) Auto price and output levels:
> Own quantity sold, by firm and size class
> Own average price, by firm and size class
> Import Quantity and Price
> Average price of all other domestic cars, for each firm and size class;

(3) Factor Costs:
> Industry-wide cost of unionized labor
> Capacity Utilization
> Exchange Rates
> Firm-specific labor costs
> Firm-specific capital costs.

The quarterly data were collected, unless otherwise noted below, for the period 1971:I to 1986:III. The macroeconomic, price and factor cost data were all expressed in real terms where appropriate. There were four U.S.-based auto assemblers included in the study: General Motors

(GM), Ford (F), Chrysler (C) and American Motors (AM). The sources for and construction of each of these data series are discussed in the next three sections.

A. Macroeconomic Variables

The major macroeconomic data series used in this study were all obtained from *Citibase: Citibank Economic Database*, a machine readable secondary source. The primary source for each series used will be noted with its description.

1. Implicit Price Deflators

The Gross National Product Implicit Price Deflator for Personal Consumption expenditures, labeled GDFC in this study, was used throughout to convert nominal values into real figures.[1] The deflator for personal consumption expenditures was chosen over the aggregate GNP deflator because the largest group of auto purchasers are private individuals, not businesses or governments. The personal consumption deflator was also used to estimate the rate of inflation in the preceding year, as described below.

2. Gross National Product

The level of the Gross National Product (GNP) was used as the income variable in this study.[2] GNP was chosen over disposable (after tax) income because both consumers and businesses consume automobiles, and pre-tax income is a better predictor of the determinants of the combined behavior of both groups. GNP was converted to real values and its logarithmic value is referred to as LOGGNP8 in the following chapters.

3. Gasoline Prices

The gasoline price component of the Consumer Price Index for All Urban Consumers (CPI-U) was used to measure the effects of fuel costs on auto demand.[3] This subcomponent of the CPI was chosen over actual average gasoline prices because the data for average gas prices was not published by the U.S. Department of Labor prior to 1974 (1978 for unleaded gas).[4] The real price of gasoline is referred to below as LOGGASP8.

4. Interest Rates

Interest rates effect the auto industry through their impact on the cost of capital for auto producers, the cost of investing in vehicles (for business use) and the cost of consumer installment credit used for auto purchases. It would be impossible to use two or three separate market interest rate series in a regression study because of problems with multicollinearity. The cost of FHA-insured mortgage interest loans (FYFHA) was chosen for this study, because it reflects the types of risk-premia associated with medium-to-long-term consumer loans for durable goods, and because a consistent time series was not available for the cost of consumer installment credit used for auto purchases.[5]

A major conceptual problem is encountered in imputing real interest rates from observed nominal rates. In theory:

(1) $$i_r = i_n - \dot{P}_e$$

where i_r is the imputed real interest rate, i_n is the observed nominal interest rate (FYFHA in this case) and $\dot{P}_e$ is the expected rate of inflation over the life of the loan.[6] Expected inflation is an unobserved variable. In this study it is assumed that consumers expect inflation in the future $\dot{P}_e$ to equal inflation levels actually experienced in the past four quarters. The inflation rate over the last 4 quarters is calculated using the implicit price deflator for personal consumption expenditures (GDFC) described above.[7]

5. Time Trend and Structural Dummy Variables

A time trend (TIME) was included in each equation to capture structural shifts in the patterns of demand and supply, at the firm/size class level. TIME is an index number series, which increases by one unit in each period. The estimated coefficient for TIME is the compound trend rate of unexplained growth or decay in the dependent variable. Four dummy variables were used to estimate the effects of gas crises in the 1970s and the VRAs in the 1980s. *G1* and *G2* test for demand shifts resulting from the sharp increases in gasoline prices which occurred in 1974 and 1979. *VRA* measures the initial, or short-run response to the initiation of the Voluntary export restraints. VRA takes on the value of 1 beginning in 1980:IV, and 0 before then.[8] *VRA1* measures long-run adjustments to the VRAs, and the effects of the relaxation of import limits which first occurred in April, 1984.[9]

B. Auto Output and Price Levels

1. Own Quantity Sold, by Firm and Size Class

The first step in developing price and output series was to classify the models built by U.S.-based assemblers into size/quality-classes. Sales data are available for 50 to 100 models (produced by the four domestic manufacturers) for the period covered by this study. Each of these models is assigned to one of five size/quality classes each year by *Ward's Automotive Yearbook:* Subcompact, compact, intermediate, full-sized and luxury. To reduce the number of equations estimated these groups were consolidated into 3 broader groups. Small cars include both subcompacts and compacts. The intermediate class is identical to that used in *Ward's*. The large class includes both full-sized and luxury cars. Luxury cars were assigned to the large class on the basis of price (usually higher) regardless of physical dimensions. Thus some of the luxury cars are small sports models, such as the Chevrolet Corvette.

The number of units sold (Dealer Sales) of each of these models in the U.S. are reported on a monthly basis in two trade publications, *Automotive News* and *Ward's Automotive Reports.* Dealer Sales were aggregated within a size class and calendar quarter for each of the four U.S.-based firms in this study (General Motors, Ford, Chrysler, and American Motors) to calculate the Q_{ij} used in this study. The index i represents size classes and j represents individual firms. The sales data were primarily collected from *Automotive News,* and *Ward's Automotive Reports* were used to cover and check omissions and errors in the Automotive News data.

Most of the quantity data used in the regression model of this study (chapters V and VI) were seasonally adjusted, using a moving average formula, to eliminate noise in the data and to conserve degrees of freedom in the regression analyses by eliminating the need for quarterly dummy variables.[10] The quantity data for American Motors could not be seasonally adjusted because there were periods in which there were no reported sales in each of the size classes, making it impossible to construct meaningful moving averages for the remaining observations in these series.

2.   *Own Average Price, by Firm and Size Class*

Published **wholesale** price data were used in this study, as a measure of manufacturer revenue per unit. Wholesale prices are regularly reported by two publications. The *Kelley Blue Book New Car Price Manual*, an industry publication generally available only to members of the automobile trade, is the primary published source for wholesale (and suggested retail) prices. A consistent historical series of the *Kelley Blue Books* is not available in any public library in the U.S.[11], thus the price data used in this study was obtained from the *Edmund's New Car Prices*, which is apparently derived from the *Kelley Blue Books.*[12]

Although prices may be adjusted several times a year for any one model, new prices are generally set for all models at the beginning of the model year (in October), or when a new model is introduced. In this study it was assumed that manufacturers set prices once per year, maintain those prices for the rest of the year, and adjust output to attain market equilibrium. There are two inherent problems with using wholesale prices which must be acknowledged. First, it is standard practice for manufacturers to rebate 1% to 3% of the wholesale price of a car to the dealer at the end of the model year if the car is sold. Often referred to as the "holdback", the extent of this payment may vary with the size of the dealer.[13] Second, the effects of manufacturer rebates were not considered in this study, because their systematic analysis would have required exhaustive examination of the trade literature. It may be possible to capture the general effects of rebates with careful use of dummy variables, in future research.

Wholesale prices are often published for a number of different versions of each particular model. The different versions, numbering from 2 to 20 for each model, generally range from basic (no-frills) to luxurious configurations with a wide spread in prices.[14] Up to 300 different model-variations have been offered by U.S.-based manufacturers in some recent years (as compared with the 50 to 100 models for which quantity data is published). In this study, the *median* price for non-station wagon versions[15] of each model was used as the representative wholesale price for each of the 50 to 100 models for which quantity data were available.[16] Non-standard optional equipment was not included in the median wholesale price, nor was it considered here.

P_{ij} or average revenue for each firm and size class was calculated as a weighted average in each quarter:

$$(2) \qquad P_{ij} = \frac{\sum_m P_{ijm} Q_{ijm}}{\sum_m Q_{ijm}}$$

where the subscript m is indexed over the models in each size class, for each firm. This measure of average revenue within size class varies over the model year because of changes in the composition of sales within a class. Nominal average revenue estimates were converted to real values by dividing through with the personal consumption expenditures deflator (GDFC).[17]

Wholesale prices were available for most domestic models in each year of the study. Price data were often not available for new car models for the first year of their production.[18] Sales of these models *were* included in the figures for Q_{ij}, but they were excluded from the calculations of average revenue, P_{ij}. This procedure implicitly assumes that average revenue obtained for new cars equaled average revenue for older models within a given firm/size class. Because new models represent a very small fraction of total sales in most of the observations, this assumption does not introduce significant distortion in the data.

3. Import Quantity and Price

A monthly time series for the total quantity of cars imported into the U.S. was obtained from *Citibase*, and was converted into quarterly form for use in this study.[19] The natural logarithm of total import car sales is labeled LOGQIMP below.

Wholesale import prices were estimated only for Japanese cars in this study, in order to focus on the impact of the VRAs on the revenues of these producers. Had other imported vehicles been included in the price index, the effects of the VRAs would have been obscured by the development of new, low cost export sources such as Korea and Yugoslavia during the period of the restraints. Import prices are not used as a determinant of the number of imports sold in the model used in this study (Chapter V), which eliminates problems with errors in variables which would arise using price and quantity data of different types in a standard demand-curve estimation.

The average wholesale price of japanese imports was estimated by dividing the total value of U.S. auto imports for consumption from Japan (as reported in the official statistics of the U.S. Dept. of Commerce) by the total quantity (number of units) of such cars imported.[20] These data were only available on a annual (calendar year) basis, so it was assumed in the model that prices are set annually (consistent with the assumptions for domestic prices). Thus the import price series has identical values in each quarter of any given calendar year. Nominal average revenue estimates were converted to real values by dividing through with the personal consumption expenditures deflator (GDFC).[21] The natural logarithm of this real price index is referred to, below, as LOGPIMP.

4. Average Price of All Other Domestic Cars, for Each Firm and Size Class

The average price of all other domestic cars was calculated using an expression similar to equation 2, above:

$$(3) \quad PBARxyy = \frac{\sum_i \sum_j P_{ij} Q_{ij}}{\sum_i \sum_j Q_{ij}} \quad \textit{for all i,j except } i = x \\ \textit{and } j = yy,$$

where x refers to a particular size class and yy refers to a particular firm. This index is used as a component of P_j, the price of all other cars, in the model estimated in Chapter V.

C. Factor Costs

1. Industry-Wide Cost of Unionized Labor

Labor contracts in the auto industry generally cover a period of three model years, and wages and benefits are usually adjusted once each year under terms of the contract. The total cost of labor to the manufacturer includes direct wages, fringe benefits and social security contributions. The cost of fringe benefits has been growing more rapidly than hourly wages so it is important to consider total costs when estimating the effects of union wage rates on output and prices. An annual estimate of the total cost of hourly labor for the 1971-1986 period was obtained from the United Auto Workers.[22] It was assumed that UAW labor costs were constant in each quarter of the model year.

2. Capacity Utilization

Because automobile production is a capital-intensive manufacturing process, it is assumed that capacity utilization levels will affect the level of marginal costs in the industry and thus output and pricing behavior. Capacity utilization levels in the U.S. auto assembly industry were obtained from *Citibase* for use in this study, and are referred to as CAPU371 in the following chapters.[23]

3. Exchange Rates

Changes in currency exchange rates will affect the costs of vehicles and components imported into the U.S., thus affecting the supply behavior of U.S. producers. The nominal U.S./Japanese exchange rate (measured in U.S. cents per Japanese Yen) was also obtained from *Citibase* and the logarithm of this series is referred to as LOGEXRJ in the following chapters.[24]

4. Firm-Specific Labor Costs

White collar wage rates, non-U.S. labor costs, non-union labor costs for production workers and the share of those other workers in a company's total labor force, as well as the UAW wage rate, will influence the cost of labor in each firm in this study. There are large differences in the level of vertical integration and the degree of internationalization among the four firms considered in this study. As a result, firm-specific labor costs differ significantly.

Annual labor costs and total employment levels for each company in this study were obtained from Standard and Poor's Compustat Services (and were used to determine total firm-specific labor costs per employee-year).[25] It was assumed that non-union wage rates and bonuses are determined annually and remain constant over the calendar year. Real wages were calculated using the deflator for personal consumption expenditures and are referred to below as REALWyy, where yy refers to one of the four companies in this study.

5. Firm-specific Cost of Capital

A measure of the annual weighted average cost of equity and borrowed capital was computed for each firm from data furnished by Standard and Poor's Compustat Services. It was assumed that the cost of capital varies across firms because of differences in risk, debt/equity ratios, and access to unique sources of financing (such as auto installment credit operations). Furthermore, since dividend payments are included in this measure, it also reflects the overall profitability of the firm and hence its market power and/or position. It was assumed that significant changes in dividend payments and borrowing costs occur only once in a calendar year and that the firm-specific cost of capital is constant within each year. The formula used to compute the firm-specific cost of capital was:

$$\textbf{(4)} \qquad REALRyy = \frac{(int_{yy} + dp_{yy} + dc_{yy})}{(pk_{yy} + ca_{yy} + cl_{yy})} - \dot{P}_e \, ,$$

where:

int_{yy} = total interest expense
dp_{yy} = dividends -- preferred
dc_{yy} = dividends -- common
pk_{yy} = property, plant and equipment -- total (gross)
ca_{yy} = current assets -- total
cl_{yy} = current liabilities -- total for company yy.[26]

D. Output Shares and Prices in the U.S. Automobile Market

The data collected for this study provide some new insights into the problems of and conditions in the U.S. auto industry. Both the quantity and price data provide new details on the nature of the problems facing this industry. Some of the most important factors affecting the auto industry (the energy crises, rising import competition) have resulted in substantial shifts in demand patterns in the U.S. auto market. Domestic producers have pursued different marketing and product mix strategies in response to changes in the domestic environment, with significant effects on firm profitability and even the viability of the U.S. auto industry as a whole.

1. Quantity Data and Shifting Demand Patterns

Standard industry statistics on the patterns of demand for cars of various size classes, as reported in the *Automotive News* Market Data Book[27] and industry trade publications (e.g. Motor Vehicle Manufacturers Association (1987)), cover sales by size class for domestic manufacturers *only*. Import sales are omitted from such statistics, which can create the mistaken impression that small car sales are a relatively small fraction of total demand. The failure to include imports in size class figures also tends to understate the magnitude of shifts in demand patterns which have resulted from changes in the U.S. economic environment in the 1970s and 1980s, as import penetration has increased.

Figure 1 summarizes the changes in market shares, by size class of car, over the 1971-1986 period for the total U.S. market, with imports included in small car sales. It appears, from the data, that the gasoline shortages and price increases which occurred in 1973 and 1979 had substantial and complex effects on the patterns of car demand. The initial effect of the 1973 gas crisis was to dramatically increase small car demand. However, this effect was short lived. The small car market share hit a mid-70s peak in 1975, when small car demand began to be displaced by demand for intermediates. The market share of large cars generally declined throughout the 1970s and 1980s.

The second gasoline crisis affected the market in a very different fashion. By the late 1970s manufacturers had down-sized their product lines and consumers had grown accustomed to smaller cars, whose market share began rising again even before 1979. After the second oil shock, the market share of small cars rose very dramatically, and the increase was sustained through 1986 (although there were slight upturns in the share of larger cars in 1982 and 1983, when gas prices fell again). Experience with higher gasoline prices, exposure to smaller

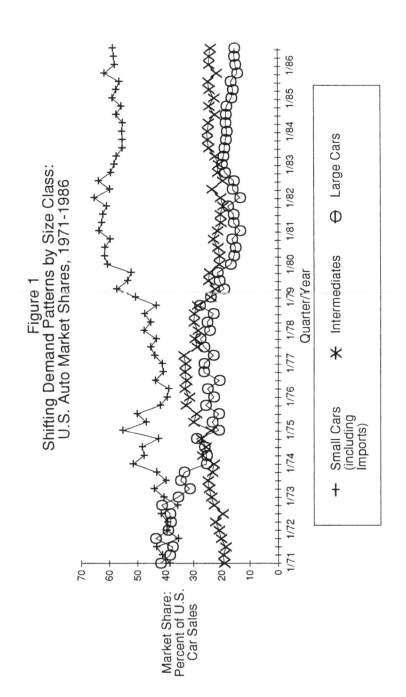

Figure 1
Shifting Demand Patterns by Size Class:
U.S. Auto Market Shares, 1971-1986

vehicles and changes in vehicle design have apparently produced a permanent shift in the pattern of demand in the U.S., in Figure 1, which appears insensitive to short-run declines in fuel costs. The market share of small cars was well in excess of 50% throughout the 1980s, despite the VRAs and the steady decline of gas prices to real levels comparable to those of the early 1970s in 1986 (Figure 2). The major U.S. auto producers responded to these shifting demand patterns in fundamentally different ways. These strategic differences have important implications for the competitiveness of these firms, and for the U.S. as a location for auto production. Table 1 reveals that prior to the second gas crisis Ford and G.M. had similar small car output shares, while Ford had the largest concentration in intermediates and G.M. had the highest large car share. While this was a profitable market position for GM in the short-run (per unit profits are highest for large cars), it ill positioned G.M. for the changes to come in the late 1970s.

TABLE 1
Output Composition, by Firm
(Percent of Domestic Firm Sales, by Size Class)

Model Year:	1977	1980	1986
Small Cars:			
G.M.	26.7%	37.9%	36.2%
Ford	22.2%	57.5%	50.6%
Chrysler	49.3%	62.4%	63.7%
Intermediates:			
G.M.	36.9%	34.4%	36.2%
Ford	49.4%	22.9%	28.9%
Chrysler	32.4%	22.2%	34.9%
Large Cars:			
G.M.	36.4%	27.7%	27.5%
Ford	28.4%	19.6%	20.5%
Chrysler	18.3%	15.4%	1.4%

As small car demand accelerated in the late 1970s, Ford followed the market, as did Chrysler, building on their existing experience in this sector. GM's response was weaker than Ford's. As a result, GM's share of the total domestic auto market fell in the 1980s, while Ford's rose until 1985 (when the VRAs were relaxed and Japanese imports rose by 25%), as shown in Figure 3. Chrysler's market share rose throughout the 1980s. The decline in GM's market share also contributed to its weak profit performance, relative to Ford and Chrysler, in this period.

In order to completely explain changes in firm-level profits it would be necessary to analyze data on unit profit levels and to examine changes in costs over time. While this type of comprehensive assessment is beyond the scope of this study, the data assembled allow

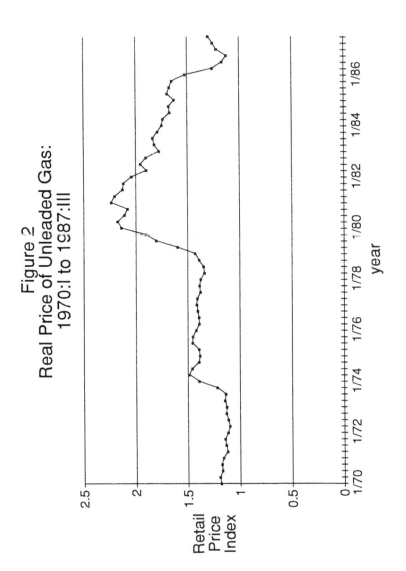

Figure 2
Real Price of Unleaded Gas:
1970:I to 1987:III

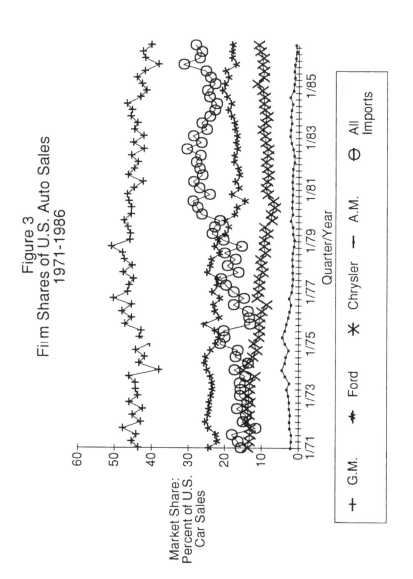

Figure 3
Firm Shares of U.S. Auto Sales
1971-1986

for more precise explanation of the changes in output and prices which occurred under the VRAs. These are the primary issues addressed in Chapters V and VI, below. However, before proceeding with model estimation it is useful to review some of the price data assembled here, to establish general trends.

2. *Price Trends and Strategic Behavior*

Estimated wholesale prices (measured in constant 1982 dollars) for the three major makers of domestic small cars and for all Japanese imports are shown in Figure 4[28]. Several trends stand out in this figure. Overall, real prices grew at a compound rate of 2.5% per year for GM small cars, over the 1971 to 1986 period. The prices of other domestic small cars were very highly correlated with those of GM. The price hikes were concentrated in three periods. The first major price increase was associated with the initial OPEC embargo, reflected in higher prices for the 1975 model year. The second shift occurred in the 1981 model year, which may have reflected the costs of additional pollution control equipment, the anticipation of auto import controls (announced in April, 1981) leading to an expected increase in import prices, or a lagged response to higher energy prices in 1979. The third shift, in 1986, was associated with the dramatic increase in prices of Japanese imports resulting from the decline of the U.S. dollar in 1985.

The higher overall degree of price coordination, particularly in periods of substantial price increases, is remarkable. These data may reflect price leadership behavior, as it is the common practice in the industry for firms to announce prices on slightly different dates, providing opportunities for other firms to adjust price accordingly. Another interesting relationship is the recent sensitivity to import prices, reflected in the 1986 jump in the prices of GM, and to a lesser extent Ford, small cars. Import prices tend to be slightly lower than the prices of domestic small cars for most of this period, in part because of differences in model mix in the two groups (with a larger proportion of subcompacts among imports).[29]

Real intermediate prices, shown in Figure 5, also grew at a compound rate of 2.5% per year. Intermediate prices were roughly 11% higher than small car prices, in both 1971 and 1986 (GM cars). The correlation between the prices of the three domestic firms is lower for intermediates than for small car prices.[30] GM prices in this class tend to be slightly lower than those of the other makers, and the gap between GM and Ford exceeds $1,000 for long periods in the late 1970s and again in the mid-1980s. In this case, Ford may be the long-term price leader. GM's prices periodically catch up to the Ford price level, only to have Ford's prices rise again in two to three years.

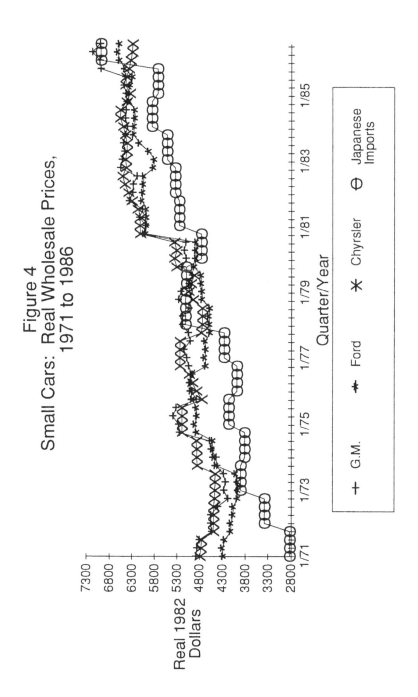

Figure 4
Small Cars: Real Wholesale Prices,
1971 to 1986

Average large-car prices (Figure 6), grew at 3.4% per year, somewhat faster than the growth rates in the other size classes.[31] As a result the price gap between large cars and all others grew during this period. In 1971 the average wholesale price of a large GM car was 44% higher than the price of a GM small car. By 1986 this gap had widened to about 64%. The gap for Ford cars was even wider, since the average large-sized Ford was more expensive than the average GM large car. Price coordination between Ford and GM was quite close, although there are again suggestions of large car price leadership at Ford in these data. Chrysler, on the other hand, pursued an independent price path in this sector, reflecting, in part, its very small share of this market segment.

The price figures suggest that in each product market the domestic firms employed strategies to closely coordinating prices. There is remarkably little variance in the price data, aside from long-run trends, and there are very few discernable periods of long-term (year-to-year) price declines. Competition appears to have been carefully managed in these markets. There is no evidence of price wars in these data for annual base prices, even in the relatively competitive market for small cars. The absence of price wars is surprising given the extreme changes in sales which are common in the auto market, due to the highly cyclical nature of durable goods demand and the capital intensive nature of production. These data suggest that price competition in this market was limited because of the oligopololistic behavior of domestic auto producers.

The pricing behavior of the domestic auto makers in 1986 illustrates the important effect that market structure can have on trade and output patterns. When the cost of imports rose, so did domestic prices. As a result, the devaluation of the dollar in the mid-1980s had little effect on the quantity of auto imports. If the domestic industry were more competitive, and exercised more price restraint, then the demand for imports might have been more sensitive to changes in the exchange rate. Hence, in this sector the dollar's devaluation worsened the trade balance (due to the increase in the cost of imports) through 1988 relative to the trade deficit in autos in 1985 (Table 2, Chapter II, above). If this pricing pattern is sustained in the long-run, further devaluations may only serve to increase the U.S. trade deficit in autos. Thus a trade (currency valuation) policy which ignores market structure may be doomed to failure.

Hypotheses about the effects of market structure on the performance of the U.S. auto industry will be examined further in the following chapters.

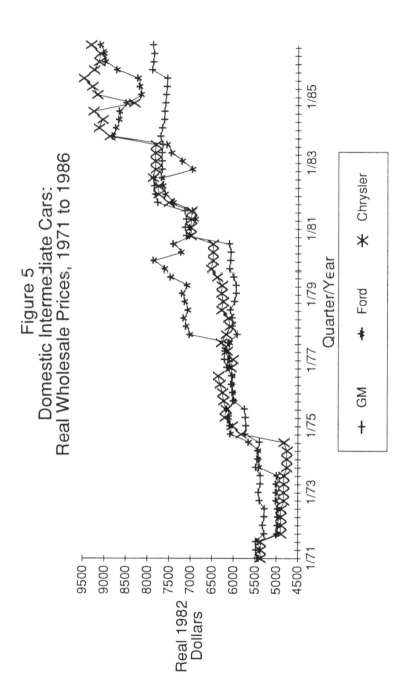

Figure 5
Domestic Intermediate Cars:
Real Wholesale Prices, 1971 to 1986

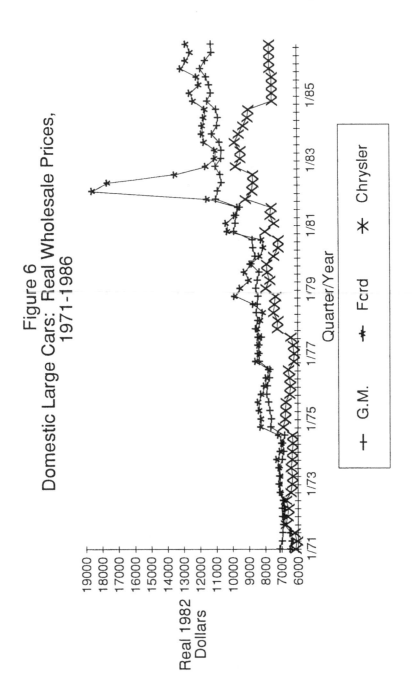

Figure 6
Domestic Large Cars: Real Wholesale Prices,
1971-1986

NOTES

1. This is a seasonally adjusted, fixed weight index which uses 1982 as a base year. U.S. Dept. of Commerce, Bureau of Economic Analysis, *National Income and Product Accounts of the U.S., 1929-84*, from various issues of the *Survey of Current Business*.

2. *ibid.*

3. This is a seasonally adjusted index, published monthly. Its values were averaged for each quarter in this study. U.S. Dept. of Labor, Bureau of Labor Statistics, *Consumer Price Index.*

4. Four different versions of the CPI (seasonally adjusted and unadjusted, wage earner index and all urban consumers index) were all compared with the two average gasoline price series (leaded regular, beginning in 1974 and unleaded regular in 1978). The index selected had the highest correlation coefficient with the available data for unleaded gasoline prices, in excess of .99.

5. The Federal Reserve Board of Governors does collect an unpublished series on consumer interest rates for car loans, but the series begins in mid-1971.

6. Dornbusch and Fischer (1987), p.303.

7. The real interest rate estimated using the procedure described in this section seems to provide reasonable values. In 1971 and 1972 the Estimated real rate is in the range of 3-5%. The real rate falls into a range between 0 and 4% between 1973 and the third quarter of 1980 (with one period of negative real rates). The estimated real rate period of negative real rates). The estimated real rate ranges between 8 and 10.9%, with a peak in 1982:II, and then falls into the 7-8% range in 1986.

In general, the procedure used here probably tends to overestimate the real rate during periods when inflation is surging, and underestimate it when the rate of inflation is abating. However, the general trends described above do tend to reflect periods of relatively loose and tight money growth rates, particularly the period of restricted monetary growth which was instituted by Paul Volker in November 1979, which lasted through most of 1985.

8. The VRAs were formally enacted in April of 1981 and tariffs on Japanese truck imports were effectively increased in August of 1980 (endnote 27 of Chapter II). Review of the price data reported in Chapter III suggests that domestic auto manufacturers substantially increased prices in the 1981 model year (which begins in 1980:IV). This shift probably reflected both higher imported truck prices due to the increase in tariffs on small Japanese trucks, and the anticipated effects of auto import controls which were known to be under consideration in 1980.

This study assumes that the price of autos imported from Japan are adjusted annually, beginning in the first quarter of each year. Thus the variable VRA takes on the value of 1 beginning in 1981:I in the import-car estimations, one period later than in the domestic equations.

9. See endnote 26 in Chapter II, for a review of the VRA limits.

10. The SAMA routine in the TSP package (version 4.1b) was used to seasonally adjust the quantity data for use in regression analysis.

11. The Los Angeles Public Library claimed to have a complete historical set of the *Kelley Blue Books*, but use of this collection was prohibited by a major fire in 1986, just prior to the initiation of this research.

12. *Edmund's New Car Prices* is published irregularly, about 5 or 6 times per year, as is the *Kelley Blue Book*. The publication dates for the *Edmund's* volumes generally lag 2-3 months behind those of the *Kelley Blue Book*, and the prices reported by *Edmund's* are identical to those reported earlier in the *Blue Book*. The Library of Congress maintains the historical collection of *Edmund's New Car Prices* used in this study.

13. The holdback effect does not present a substantial econometric problem if the holdback is relatively constant over time, since it would have the effect of multiplying all prices (or all coefficients in an estimated price regression) by a coefficient on the order of .98.

14. For example, the basic 1980 Ford LTD was produced in 8 versions (including 3 station wagons) ranging from the LTD-S (4 door) with a wholesale base price of $5,058 to the Country Squire Wagon with a wholesale price of $5,943. The median price, non-station wagon LTD was the LTD Sedan (4-door) with a base price of $5,329 in 1980 *(Edmund's New Car Prices, 1980)*. The prices used in this study did not

include dealer freight or "participatory advertising" charges, nor any state or local taxes.

15. Station wagons were omitted from the price survey because they are a relatively small share of total sales (5% to 11% of total new car registrations in the U.S. during the 71-86 period, according to *Ward's 1987 Automotive Yearbook*, p.138). Station wagons are generally priced several (10% to 20%) times higher than comparable sedan versions of the same model, so their inclusion could bias median prices upwards in a misleading fashion.

16. High and Low prices were also collected for each model, but were not used in this study.

17. In order to eliminate unwarranted variation in these series the average value of the deflator (GDFC), over the model year, was used to convert from nominal to real values.

18. There were also instances when prices were unavailable for old models as they were phased out of production. These models were generally assumed to have wholesale prices equal to those prevailing for the same model in the preceding model year for which there was data. Since the quantity data are for *dealer* sales this is a reasonable assumptions because it may take a number of months for dealers to dispose of remaining inventory of discontinued models.

19. The primary source of the import quantity data is U.S. Dept. of Commerce, Bureau of Economic Analysis, as reported in the *Survey of Current Business*. This series covers sales of all "foreign-type cars", and is not seasonally adjusted. The *Citibase* label for this series is RCAR6F. The *Citibase* series RCAR6T (total U.S. car sales) and RCAR6D (total sales of domestic car models) are also used in summarizing domestic output in the final section of this chapter. These summary statistics are identical to the dealer sales figures published by *Automotive News* and *Ward's Automotive Reports*.

20. These figures are reported by the U.S. International Trade Commission, *The U.S. Automobile Industry: Monthly Report on Selected Economic Indicators* (Report to the Subcommittee on Trade, Committee on Ways and Means, under investigation number 332-207 under section 332 of the Tariff Act of 1930), Washington, D.C., USITC, various issues.

21. In order to eliminate unwarranted variation in this series the average value of the deflator (GDFC), over the calendar year, was used to convert from nominal to real values.

22. Private communication, United Autoworkers Research Dept., July 1988.

23. The citibase code for the capacity utilization in S.I.C. code industry 371 is IPX371. The original source for this series, which is a seasonally adjusted quarterly index, is the U.S. Dept. of Commerce. Bureau of Economic Analysis, *News Release on Capacity Utilization* (various issues).

24. This is a monthly data series (Citibase code EXRJAN) representing an average of daily rates. The monthly values in each quarter were averaged for use in this study. The original source for this series is the Board of Governors of the Federal Reserve System, *Foreign Exchange Rates, G.5(405)*.

25. Standard and Poor's Compustat Services, Inc., *Compustat Annual Tapes*. Compustat annual data are collected from the published financial reports of publicly traded companies. Firm specific labor costs (W_i) were computed as the ratio of labor and related expenses (Compustat data item 42) to total employees (Compustat data item 7).

26. *ibid.* Corresponding data item numbers from Compustat (in parentheses) are int_{yy} (15), dp_{yy} (19), dc_{yy} (21), pk_{yy} (7), ca_{yy} (4), and cl_{yy} (5).

27. The *Market Data Book* is published annually, in the last week of April, as a regular issue of *Automotive News*.

28. The price data reported in Figure 4 are weighted average values, as calculated in Section B (Chapter IV).

29. Note that import and domestic "price" referred to here are not strictly comparable, since import prices are the average values at the port of entry and domestic are prices are the weighted average dealer costs for small cars.

30. The price correlation matrix is presented in chapter VI.

31. Note that the vertical (price) range is much larger in Figure 5 than in Figures 3 and 4, in order to accommodate the Ford price outlier in 1981, which may convey the mistaken impression that Large car prices grew slowly. The 1981 Ford prices reflect a transition period in which Lincoln Continentals were the only large Fords sold, because of transitions to new models in the other Ford lines.

CHAPTER V
MODEL ESTIMATION

This chapter is an empirical study of the ways in which import protection, in the form of the VRAs, affected output and prices in the U.S. auto market. The models used take into account the structure of the domestic industry and assess its impact on outcomes, or performance, in this market. The VRAs affected the levels of sales and production in the U.S., and the level of wages and profits in the domestic auto industry.[1] Regression techniques are used here to estimate these effects, for each of the U.S.-based auto producers (over 3 size-classes of cars), for auto imports and for factor costs. Chapter VI then develops a simulation model which takes into account the interactions of each of these stakeholders in determining the number of autos sold, the average prices of cars sold in the U.S. and total employment in the U.S. auto industry, with and without the VRAs.

The empirical analysis presented here will show that the VRAs had significant effects on domestic prices and sales, in all three classes of cars considered (small, medium and large cars). It also appears that each of the U.S. based producers responded differently to the quotas, which implies that firm strategy and market power/position considerations were important factors in determining the way in which the VRAs affected the domestic industry. The domestic industry is a tight oligopoly[2], and it responded to protection primarily by raising prices, and thus profits while the VRAs were in effect in the 1981-86 period. However, the VRAs were not enacted in a policy vacuum, and the investigation in this chapter will show that the VRAs were only one of several significant government policies which brought about changes in the behavior of domestic auto producers. The most important of these were apparently the Corporate Auto Fuel Economy (CAFE) standards and the "Gas Guzzler" tax.

A. Fuel Economy Regulations

There are two different federal laws designed to increase fleet fuel economy. Each creates different incentives for changes in the mix of models produced in the U.S. The first, and most important, is the Corporate Auto Fuel Economy (CAFE) standard which was established in The Energy Policy and Conservation Act of 1975. The CAFE standard is an increasing restrictive set of minimum standards for the average fuel efficiency of all autos sold by any one firm in the U.S. in a given model year. The initial standards were set at 18, 19 and 20 piles per gallon (mpg) for auto model years 1978, 1979 and 1980 respectively, and the standard was set to rise to 27.5 mpg beginning in 1985 (Henderson, 1985). A fine of $5 per car for every tenth of a mile per gallon shortfall is assessed for every car sold in a given year by any firm which fails to meet the standard. Firm's may earn credits for exceeding the standards, and may carry credits forward or backward for 3 years, making it possible to postpone fine payments for at least 3 years after missing the target, even if a firm has no credits available at the time the target was missed.

The CAFE rules are applied separately to cars produced domestically and to those a firm imports. The CAFE rules create substantial incentives which encourage domestic firms to produce small cars in the U.S., because of their extensive production of large, inefficient cars in the U.S. The CAFE rules also discourage "captive imports" by U.S. firms with substantial sales of large cars, prompting Dan Luria to argue that "CAFE acts like a domestic content law (Henderson, 1986, p. 46)". In response to these new rules Chrysler adopted a unique strategic response, eliminating many large cars from its model lines and downsizing others, "raising its average fuel economy from 21.7 mpg to 26.1 mpg in one year, 1981 (*ibid*)". In 1986 fines of $386 million were pending against GM and $24 million against Ford for violating the CAFE standards in earlier years (*The Wall Street Journal* October 3, 1986, p. 58), but they were hoping to avoid paying these fines by earning credits for exceeding the standard at some point in the future.

GM and Ford first failed to meet the CAFE standards in the years 1983 through 1985. They used prior credits to offset potential fines in 1983 and 1984 and then incurred the fines noted above in 1985.[3] The Dept. of Transportation then relaxed the CAFE standards to 26 mpg for the years 1986 though 1988 (*The Wall Street Journal*, October 2, 1985 and October 3, 1986) and the standard is presently set to increase to 27.5 mpg in 1990.

The second significant fuel economy regulation is the "gas guzzler" tax, which was enacted as part of the Energy Tax Act of 1978. In 1986 this tax is applied to cars with a mileage rating of less than 22.5 mpg and ranged from a (manufacturer paid) tax of $500 for a car with a mileage rating between 21.5 and 22.5 mpg to $3,850 on any car getting less than 12.5 mpg.[4] These taxes only generated about $4 million per year in revenues for the U.S. government, by 1983,[5] suggesting that they applied primarily to low-volume imports such as the Rolls Royce. This tax clearly creates an incentive for manufacturers to downsize, eliminate full-sized model lines and raise large car prices. It does not create any incentives to expand domestic production. Crandall, *et al* (1986) show that the CAFE standards and Gas Guzzler tax put substantial upward pressure on the prices of large cars by 1984.[6] This conclusion is confirmed in this chapter, and the policy measures in effect in the early 1980s are also shown to substantially reduced total large car output. Chapter VI will consider whether this result was caused by the VRAs, by fuel economy regulations, or by both.

The empirical specifications and estimation techniques used are discussed in the next section. Results in each size class of cars are then discussed and the chapter closes with an analysis of the effects of the VRAs on wages rates and capital costs in the industry.

B. Estimation

1. Empirical Specifications

a. Firm Specific Price and Output Levels. In Chapter III the residual demand curve facing an individual producer in the U.S. auto industry was derived. The structure of this model and the factor cost submodels will be reviewed here and then the specifications for estimation will be presented in Section 2.

It is assumed that automakers set prices, for each of three size classes of cars, once each model year and then allow quantities to adjust to clear the market. Firm-specific demand (U.S. sales of a given size class, in a given period,(Q_i) depends on the firm's own price (P_i), the prices of its competitors (P_j), a vector of macroeconomic and structural variables (Y), and on the costs of production for its competitors (which will affect the quantities supplied by other producers):

(1) $$Q_i = f(P_i, P_j, Y, W, W_l)$$

where W is a vector of industry wide factor costs and W_l is a vector of firm-specific factor costs for firms other than firm i. The estimated parameters of firm i's residual demand curve will reflect the reactions of other firms in the industry to changes in firm i's price level.

Each firm is assumed to set output by equating marginal cost with marginal revenue:

$$(2) \qquad MC_i(Q_i, W, W_i) = Q_i + P_i g(P_i, P_j, W, W_i),$$

where W_i is a vector of firm specific factor costs for firm i and g is the partial derivative of equation 1 with respect to own price. Equilibrium price and output levels for firm i are determined jointly by these two equations. This specification clearly establishes that the parameters of the demand equation will be identified when there exist firm-specific cost variables W_i.

The most fundamental econometric problem posed by the system of equations 1 and 2 is that the parameters of firm i's supply function cannot be identified because every variable which affects residual demand will also appear in the supply equation, through the marginal revenue equation. Without estimates of supply behavior, it is impossible to use equations 1 and 2 to directly estimate the effects of the VRAs on output and prices in the domestic auto industry.

b. The Reduced Form Model. Price and quantities sold are estimated separately, instead of estimating the full system of demand and supply equations, using the reduced form approach developed in Chapter III. A model of the following general form is estimated for each of 3 size-classes of cars (small, medium and large) for the four U.S.-based auto assemblers (General Motors, Ford, Chrysler and American Motors(AM)[7]), and for total imports, as well:

$$(3) \qquad Q_i = m(P_j, Y, W, W_l, W_i),$$

$$(4) \qquad P_i = n(P_j, Y, W, W_l, W_i).$$

The actual variables included in the vectors P_j, Y, W, W_l and W_i will be discussed in section 2.

A reduced form model does not directly estimate residual demand elasticities, in contrast to Baker and Bresnahan's (1985) model. However, it will provide estimates of the ways in which domestic firms *responded* to the imposition of the quotas, as reflected in the effects of the quotas on output and prices in each firm/size class included in the study. Equations 3 and 4 thus form a model of outcomes or the performance of domestic firms which is determined, in part, by residual demand elasticities. Conduct and structural parameters are imbedded in the reduced form coefficients and cannot be directly evaluated using this technique.

In simplest terms, when market protection is awarded to a firm with market power, the firm will observe an outward shift in its residual demand curve. Given such a demand shift the firm can choose to increase price, quantity sold, or both. The choice of price and/or quantity will depend on the firm's market power and on the reactions of other firms to changes in its own price or output levels (as reflected in the elasticity of its residual demand curve). Thus market structure and the particular form of prevailing oligopoly conduct (if any) can be important influences over the way in which trade protection affects industry performance. The model estimated in this chapter will reveal the degree to which the VRAs affected both prices and output levels of domestic auto producers. It is entirely possible that the market power of one or more domestic producers was so enhanced by the VRAs that they caused a reduction in firm output, relative to levels that would have been achieved without protection.[8]

The model developed in equations 3 and 4 will also be applied to the market for imports. Factor markets are also assumed to have been affected by the VRAs, which will in turn have an impact on the product markets through equations 3 and 4.

c. Factor Costs. If the labor market in the auto industry is sufficiently concentrated on either the supply or the demand sides, then wages will not competitively determined. A situation in which there is significant concentration on both sides of the market can be modeled as a bilateral monopoly or oligopoly. Theoretical research on labor market structures has shown that wages will be determined by negotiations between the parties in question under conditions involving bilateral market power. In cases where product markets are also concentrated, such negotiations can result in labor's capture of a share of the monopoly profits earned in the product market. Alternatively, if labor supply curves are upward sloping a VRA-induced increase in labor demand in the domestic market would also put upward pressure on wages under a purely competitive labor market structure. In both cases a VRA-related increase in wages would have an impact on firm-specific marginal costs, and hence on output and prices. Thus wages and other factor costs are treated as endogenous variables in this model.

VRA-related changes in factor costs are a secondary channel through which these policies can effect domestic output and prices. If the VRAs resulted in higher wages, then in a competitive product market these wage effects would offset some of the (positive) effects of the VRAs on output and reinforce their (positive) effects on prices. This model will provide empirical evidence on the nature of these secondary effects in this highly concentrated industry.

The cost of capital, on a firm-specific basis, includes profit as reported annually to the SEC. Profits may be influenced by any of the factors which change the output, price, or price-cost markup of the firm. Thus profits, and hence firm-specific capital costs, may also have been affected by the VRAs.

In principle, wages and profits could be influenced by any of the variables which effect own output and price in equations 3 and 4 above. However, price variables from the right hand sides of equations 3 and 4 were omitted from the factor cost equations in order to avoid problems with non-linearities in model simulation. Factor cost equations were estimated for three groups of variables: 1) the total hourly, unionized labor cost for the three largest assembly firms in the U.S., under United Auto Worker labor contracts (a component of the Vector W); 2) the firm-specific cost (per employee year) of all labor, including union, non union and management workers (both domestic and foreign) for GM, Ford and Chrysler (a component of W_i); and 3) the firm-specific cost of capital for the same firms (another component of W_i).[9] The basic model used to estimate all factor cost (FC) equations is:

(5) $$FC_i = k(Y, W).$$

The variables included in the vectors Y and W are discussed in the next section. UAW hourly labor costs are one of the factors included in the vector W for all other FC equations. Each of these equations is estimated separately and the results are used in chapter VI to assess the direct and indirect effects of the VRAs on industry wage and profit levels in simulations of output and prices in the domestic industry under alternative scenarios.

2. Estimation Techniques

a. Price and Quantity Equations. Equations 3 and 4 are estimated in log-log form, for each of the 4 U.S.-based auto assemblers, using quarterly data for the period 1971:II through 1986:III. The quantity data in this model were seasonally adjusted for GM, Ford and Chrysler, to avoid the necessity for seasonal dummy variables. The quantity data for AM could not be seasonally adjusted, because there were periods in which AM had no sales in each of these size classes. The equations estimated are:

(6) $\quad Q_i = a_1 + \alpha_1 P_j + \alpha_2 Y + \alpha_3 W + \alpha_4 W_I + \alpha_5 W_i + \varepsilon_1,$

(7) $\quad P_i = b_1 + \beta_1 P_j + \beta_2 Y + \beta_3 W + \beta_4 W_I + \beta_5 W_i + \varepsilon_2,$

where a_i and b_i are parameters and α_i and β_i are vectors of parameters. The error terms, ε_1 and ε_2, are assumed to be uncorrelated so that the equations may be estimated separately. Equations 6 and 7 were initially estimated using ordinary least squares (OLS) techniques. It is assumed that equations 6 and 7 are independent in this reduced form approach, which is designed to eliminate problems with simultaneity which are encountered when estimating the parameters of demand curves. Under these assumptions OLS techniques will yield unbiased estimates of the structural parameters in equations 6 and 7.

The disturbances within each model may be serially correlated because of the use of time series data. OLS coefficient estimates are inefficient, and the estimated standard error terms are biased in the presence of serial correlation. The correlation of the errors (RHO) and the coefficients of each model were re-estimated using the maximum likelihood procedure suggested by Beach and McKinnon (1978). The asymptotic standard errors and t-statistics generated by the Beach/McKinnon procedure were then evaluated. The results generated using the Beach/McKinnon procedure were utilized in place of the OLS estimates when the null hypothesis of no autocorrelation could be rejected at the 20% significance level.[10] In the presentation of results in Section B, below, the estimated value of RHO and its t-statistic are reported for each equation for which the null-hypothesis of no autocorrelation was rejected.

b. Independent Variables. Equations 6 and 7 were estimated for each 3 classes of cars (small, medium and large) for the four U.S.-based auto assemblers, General Motors (GM), Ford (F), Chrysler (C) and American Motors (AM), and for imported cars.[11] A common set of variables was used in estimating these equations for each firm/size class of cars. Sources for and the construction of the variables was described in Chapter IV, above. Variables are measured in real terms where appropriate. Most of the macroeconomic and price variables were expressed in logarithmic form.

Two price variables were included in each equation: The average price of imported cars, LOGPIMP, and the average price of all other domestic cars, LGPBRxyy (where x is a size class label--S, M or L--

and yy is a firm label--GM, F, C or AM). LGPBRxyy is calculated separately for each firm/size-class to exclude own prices.

Three macroeconomic and five structural variables were included in each regression. Gross national product (LOGGNP8), Gasoline Prices (LOGGASP8) and the real interest rate (REALR) were all significant in one or more of the regressions.[12] Real interest rates are not expressed as logarithms, since they occasionally take on negative values.

A time trend (TIME) was included in each equation to capture structural shifts in the patterns of demand and supply, at the firm/size class level. TIME is an index number series, which increases by one unit in each period. The estimated coefficient for TIME is the compound rate of unexplained growth or decay in the dependent variable. Four dummy variables were used to estimate the effects of gas crises in the 1970s and the VRAs in the 1980s. *G1* and *G2* test for demand shifts resulting from the sharp increases in gasoline prices which occurred in 1974 and 1979. *VRA* measures the initial, or short-run response to the initiation of the Voluntary export restraints. VRA takes on the value of 1 beginning in 1980:IV, and 0 before then.[13] *VRA1* measures long-run adjustment to the VRAs, and the effects of the relaxation of import limits which first occurred in April, 1984.[14]

Three common cost factors were included in the model: 1) United Auto Worker total hourly compensation rates (LOGUAWC8); 2) a measure of capacity utilization in the U.S. motor vehicle industry (LOGCAPU); and 3) the nominal Japanese/U.S. exchange rate (LOGEXRJ). LOGCAPU was included to correct for the effects of scale economies and short-run output variations. LOGEXRJ was included to measure the effects of changes in the delivered cost of Japanese cars in the U.S. Finally, firm-specific costs of labor and capital were also included (REALWyy and REALRyy, where yy takes on the values GM, F and C) for the big-three U.S. assemblers. RealWyy and RealRyy constitute W_1 and W_i in each equation.

c. Factor Cost Equations. Equation 5 is estimated in log-log form, for GM, F and C, using quarterly data for the period 1971:II through 1986:III. The equations estimated are:

$$(8) \qquad FC_i = c_1 + \Gamma_1 Y + \Gamma_2 W + \varepsilon_3,$$

where c_1 is a parameter and Γ_i are vectors of parameters.

C. Results

There are 24 price and quantity equations in this model, including all domestic and foreign firms and size classes.[15] The model is completed with 7 factor cost equations. The results will be presented in 6 tables organized by size-class groups, for the domestic industry, 1 table for imports and 2 tables for factor costs. The set of variables described in the previous section was used in each of the domestic equations. There are problems with multicollinearity in the right-hand variables in these regressions. With multicollinearity the efficiency of parameter estimates is reduced, but parameter estimates are consistent. As a result, variables whose estimated parameters had low t-statistics were kept in the regressions to ensure consistency with the theoretical model.

Analysis of the results will focus on the direct response of output and prices to the imposition of the VRAs, and on the sensitivity of price and output for each firm to changes in other firms prices and to macro-economic variables. The way in which firms respond to changes in the prices of other cars (both domestic and foreign) is an important measure of how industry structure has affected performance. Overall results for each firm (aggregating over all three size classes) will then be discussed at the end of the chapter.

1. Small Domestic Cars

a. Domestic Small-Car Quantity Equations. The results of the output regressions for small cars built by U.S.-based assemblers are shown in Table 1. The direct effect of the VRAs on output was initially positive, as measured by the firm-level coefficients for the dummy variable VRA. The effect was statistically significant at the 5% level for all of the domestic producers except for GM.[16] After three years, however, the direct benefits of the VRA--calculated by summing the coefficients for VRA and VRA1--were reduced or eliminated in most cases. VRA1 captures several structural changes: long run changes in domestic output in response to protection, the decision by the Japanese government to begin relaxing the VRAs in 1984, and the rise in imports from other countries which were brought about by the VRAs (especially imports from South Korea). VRA1 is negative and statistically significant for F and AM, and the coefficient is large enough to cancel out the direct short-run benefits of the VRAs for these firms. The indirect effects of the VRAs will be examined in Chapter VI. These results are consistent with the expected effects of the VRAs, discussed in Chapters II and III.

TABLE 1

SMALL-CAR QUANTITY ESTIMATES[17]

Dependent Variable:	LOGQSGM	LOGQSF	LOGQSC	LOGQSAM
Independent Variable:	Estimated Coefficient	Estimated Coefficient	Estimated Coefficient	Estimated Coefficient
C	1.903	-14.382	-23.874	19.571
	(0.127)	(-0.777)	(1.310)	(0.698)
LOGPIMP	-1.157	0.354	-0.081	0.148
	(-3.239)	(0.748)	(-0.173)	(0.200)
LGPBRSyy	-1.072	-2.012	-0.325	-5.839
	(-1.376)	(2.130)	(0.396)	(-3.488)
LOGGNP8	4.790	4.054	3.503	3.964
	(2.694)	(1.789)	(1.566)	(1.065)
LOGGASP8	0.127	-0.913	-0.806	-0.179
	(0.395)	(-2.159)	(-1.957)	(-0.242)
REALR	-0.010	-0.017	-0.004	-0.089
	(-0.471)	(0.652)	(-0.167)	(-2.160)
TIME	-0.011	-0.008	-0.013	0.039
	(-0.758)	(-0.433)	(-0.715)	(1.336)
VRA	0.094	0.434	0.384	0.936
	(0.694)	(2.364)	(2.141)	(3.214)
VRA	0.034	-0.442	-0.158	-1.336
	(0.255)	(-2.196)	(-0.816)	(-3.567)
G1	0.108	-0.064	-0.118	0.482
	(0.474)	(-0.217)	(-0.405)	(1.080)
G2	-0.060	-0.423	0.139	-1.096
	(-0.329)	(-1.688)	(0.558)	(-2.883)
LOGUAWC8	-0.538	1.240	1.722	-1.413
	(-0.529)	(0.953)	(1.334)	(-0.534)
LOGCAPU	-1.465	1.594	2.023	0.019
	(-2.551)	(2.059)	(2.747)	(0.014)
REALWGM	0.248	1.047	0.577	0.198
	(0.379)	(1.191)	(0.646)	(0.155)
REALWF	-0.359	-4.044	-1.252	-1.776
	(-0.326)	(-2.662)	(-0.846)	(-0.768)
REALWC	0.457	1.872	-0.532	2.437
	(0.698)	(2.179)	(-0.629)	(1.898)
REALRGM	-0.498	-3.034	-0.595	-3.996
	(-0.468)	(-2.008)	(-0.396)	(-1.622)
REALRF	3.221	4.457	-1.262	32.171
	(0.826)	(0.824)	(0.237)	(3.966)
REALRC	-0.412	-3.568	2.750	-23.423
	(-0.148)	(-0.962)	(0.751)	(-4.065)
LOGEXRJ	-0.214	0.640	0.394	1.934
	(-0.731)	(1.663)	(1.039)	(3.075)
Q1DUM				-0.066
				(-0.456)
Q2DUM				-0.083
				(-0.687)
Q3DUM				-0.296
				(-2.230)
ADJUSTED R-SQUARED=	0.979	0.654	0.652	0.835
DURBIN-WATSON STATISTIC=	2.051	2.222	2.271	
F-STATISTIC (19,42)=	148.405	7.057	7.011	14.074
FINAL VALUE OF RHO=	-0.349			
T-STATISTIC FOR RHO=	-2.435			

The coefficient for the average price of other domestic cars (LGPBRSyy) is negative and statistically significant (at the 80% significance level) for 3 of the 4 firms. At first glance this result appears counter-intuitive because other cars are substitutes and increases in the prices of other cars would be expected to increase demand for the model in question. However, LGPBRSyy is very highly correlated with own price (the simple correlation coefficient averaged .93 for small cars, across the four firms, as shown below). This suggests that prices move together in this industry, and that changes in the average price level are more important than changes in relative prices in determining patterns of demand. Thus the coefficient on LGPBRSyy can be viewed as a proxy for the own price elasticity of demand.[18] From this perspective, the results are consistent with a model of a tightly coordinated oligopoly. GM's implied price elasticity is only slightly greater that 1.0, suggesting a large price/markup ratio. The implied price elasticities facing other firms rise in inverse-proportion to size for Ford and AM, in a manner consistent with the expected negative relationship between market share and the elasticity of residual demand curves.

The strong negative effect of higher average prices on the number of cars sold is a potentially important channel of indirect VRA impacts. To the extent that domestic prices were increased by the quotas the positive direct effects of the VRAs on output would be offset. This price effect is examined in chapter VI, below.

Import prices (LOGPIMP) had a small, or negative (in the case of GM) effect on domestic output, which is surprising. One possible explanation is that domestic producers simply raise prices, rather than increase output, when import manufacturers face cost increases or other supply problems. Kwoka (1984) provides anecdotal evidence in support of this view. It appears that GM, in particular, chose to raise prices rather than output in the early 1980s, when the VRAs first limited Japanese imports, as shown in the next section. The other possible explanation has to do with errors-in-variables problems. The import price data used here is a port-of-entry-based wholesale price index. It has been widely reported that the quotas had their strongest price effects at the retail level, where dealers where often charging sticker-price premiums (additional dealer markup) of up to several thousand dollars per car in the later stages of the VRAs, in some cities. The effects of the VRAs on retail import prices are not captured directly in this model (their effects on domestic output are reflected in the coefficients for the VRA dummy variables).

The level of domestic income (LOGGNP8) had significant positive effects on small car output for GM, Ford and Chrysler. Real interest rates generally had negative effects, but the coefficients were statistically insignificant. The same was true for the effect of the time trend.

Gasoline prices had a large, statistically significant and negative effect on the number of small cars sold by Ford and Chrysler. This effect also shows up as a negative, statistically significant structural shift with the second gas crisis (G2) for Ford. These results suggest that even the small cars produced by these companies had trouble competing with small, fuel efficient imports.[19] Thus the gasoline crisis is confirmed to have played a significant role in the decline of this segment of the domestic auto industry.

On the factor cost side of the model, labor costs generally had the expected negative effect on output. The costs of capital, however, had a positive and statistically significant effect on output for Ford and Chrysler. The firm-specific capital cost-output relationship should probably be viewed as a simple correlation, rather than one of cause and effect in this case. Profits tend to be procyclical in this industry, particularly for the smaller firms, and capital costs (as defined here) are thus endogenous.

Capacity utilization (LOGCAPU) is significant for GM, F and C. The positive coefficients for LOGCAPU found for Ford and Chrysler would seem to suggest that these firms face significant scale economies, although there may be reversal of cause and effect here as well, since capacity utilization is well correlated with GNP and total industry output. Finally, the Japanese/U.S. exchange rate is also significant for F and AM, as expected. Higher exchange rates push up the delivered cost of Japanese imports, which should have positive effects on the demand for domestic products.

b. Domestic Small-Car Price Equations. The results of the price regressions for small cars built by U.S.-based assemblers are shown in Table 2. The direct effects of the VRAs on prices were initially positive, as measured by the firm-level coefficients for the dummy variable VRA. The effect was statistically significant at the 5% level for all of the domestic producers except for AM. The initial direct effect on price was much smaller than the quantity effect for all producers except GM, as shown in Table 3. The coefficient on VRA is roughly proportional to the percentage change predicted in the dependent variable, *ceteris paribus*, because the variables are measured in log-log form. GM's behavior contrasts sharply with that of the rest of the industry. The VRA initially had a much stronger effect on output than price for Ford, Chrysler and AM, which was not the case for GM.

TABLE 2

SMALL-CAR PRICE ESTIMATES

Dependent Variable:	LOGPSGM	LOGPSF	LOGPSC	LOGPSAM
Independent Variable:	Estimated Coefficient	Estimated Coefficient	Estimated Coefficient	Estimated Coefficient
C	10.761	4.930	4.891	0.150
	(3.074)	(1.539)	(1.498)	(0.046)
LOGPIMP	-0.035	0.147	0.084	-0.011
	(-0.383)	(1.436)	(0.895)	(-0.123)
LGPBRSyy	0.704	0.101	0.216	-0.457
	(3.763)	(0.653)	(1.505)	(-2.371)
LOGGNP8	-0.915	0.311	0.231	0.518
	(-2.129)	(0.766)	(0.553)	(1.208)
LOGGASP8	-0.129	-0.119	-0.073	0.011
	(-1.639)	(-1.489)	(-0.929)	(0.132)
REALR	-0.005	0.001	-0.000	0.005
	(-0.958)	(0.137)	(-0.039)	(0.983)
TIME	0.008	0.001	0.000	-0.002
	(2.429)	(0.313)	(0.051)	(-0.498)
VRA	0.094	0.186	0.110	0.029
	(2.795)	(5.740)	(3.300)	(0.860)
VRA1	-0.042	0.051	0.090	-0.042
	(-1.150)	(1.077)	(2.158)	(-0.966)
G1	-0.019	0.019	-0.010	0.082
	(-0.347)	(0.353)	(-0.172)	(1.602)
G2	-0.009	0.019	0.095	-0.031
	(-0.188)	(0.384)	(1.908)	(-0.697)
LOGUAWC8	-0.224	-0.095	0.263	-0.210
	(-0.907)	(-0.427)	(1.082)	(-0.690)
LOGCAPU	-0.241	-0.293	-0.267	-0.038
	(-1.564)	(-1.632)	(-1.661)	(-0.247)
REALWGM	0.300	-0.087	-0.195	-0.067
	(1.852)	(-0.481)	(-1.123)	(-0.455)
REALWF	0.084	0.159	0.105	-0.114
	(0.295)	(0.507)	(0.347)	(-0.430)
REALWC	-0.059	-0.159	-0.290	0.224
	(-0.362)	(-0.915)	(-1.749)	(1.513)
REALRGM	-0.667	0.051	0.473	-0.183
	(-2.350)	(0.157)	(1.510)	(-0.643)
REALRF	-0.889	-1.903	-2.285	0.198
	(-0.868)	(-1.583)	(-2.059)	(0.212)
REALRC	0.776	0.182	0.231	-1.387
	(1.106)	(0.228)	(0.309)	(-2.090)
LOGEXRJ	-0.066	0.130	0.140	0.030
	(-0.906)	(1.744)	(1.898)	(0.412)
Q1DUM				0.003
				(0.179)
Q2DUM				-0.005
				(-0.392)
Q3DUM				-0.017
				(-1.109)
ADJUSTED R-SQUARED =	0.975	0.997	0.994	0.838
DURBIN-WATSON STATISTIC =	1.972	1.795	1.878	
F-STATISTIC (19,42) =	126.824	1144.130	537.029	14.404
FINAL VALUE RHO =			0.747	0.334
T-STATISTIC RHO =			7.453	2.316

In the long-run, small car prices for some firms continued to rise as a result of the VRAs, as shown by the coefficients on VRA1 for Ford and Chrysler. The total direct effect on prices in the long-run (again, found by summing the coefficients for VRA and VRA1) was positive for all of the domestic firms, except for AM. Thus the VRAs appear to have increased prices and had an insignificant direct effect on the output of small cars, in the long-run. However, it is important to note that the total impact of the VRAs consists of both direct and indirect effects. The later will be examined in Chapter VI.

Market position and firm strategy generated important differences in the way firms responded to changes in the prices of other cars. GM had a larger and more significant (1%-level) increase in its small car prices in response to an escalation in the price of other domestic cars (LGPBRSyy) than did other manufacturers. Chrysler had a smaller and less significant response, and Ford's response was insignificant. AM apparently responded to higher prices of its competitors by cutting its own small-car prices, but this probably reflects AM's overall competitive difficulties.

Firm responses to changes in import prices (LOGPIMP) had a different pattern. The effect on Ford's prices was positive and significant at the 20% level, and insignificant for the other producers. Apparently Ford was somewhat better able to compete with imports with its small car models, such as the popular Escort/Lynxx series cars, than were other U.S. based auto firms.

National income had a negative, statistically significant effect on GM prices and was insignificant in all other cases, suggesting that other factors (principally the prices of other cars) were more important determinants of the prices of domestic small cars. Gasoline prices generally had a negative effect on small car prices (significant at the 20% level for Ford and GM), confirming the view that domestically-produced small cars had trouble competing with imports when gas prices increased in the 1970s. The sole exception to this pattern was the case of the dummy variable for the second gas crisis (G2), which had a positive effect on Chrysler small car prices, which may have benefited from the inclusion in Chrysler's line of captive imports from Mitsubishi.

Real interest rates and the time trend generally had insignificant effects on prices, as did the time trend. The only exception to this pattern was the positive time trend for GM small car prices. This trend offset the tendency for GM prices to fall with GNP.

TABLE 3

THE INITIAL EFFECTS OF THE VRA ON SMALL-CAR PRICE AND QUANTITY FOR DOMESTIC MANUFACTURERS

(Coefficient for VRA Effect)

Equation for:	GM	Ford	Chrysler	AM
Quantity	.094	.434*	.384*	.936*
Price	.094*	.186*	.110*	.029

*Statistically significant at the 5% level.

Own, firm-specific wage rates had the expected positive effect on prices (significant at the 5% level for GM). The own-wage effect was negative for Chrysler, which is probably explained by the wage concessions Chrysler received as part of its government loan guarantee package in the early 1980s, at a time when small car prices were rising rapidly. Results on firm-specific capital costs were mixed, as was the case with the small car quantity regressions, for the reasons discussed in section 1a., above. Capacity utilization rates (LOGCAPU) had a negative effect (significant at the 20% level) on prices for GM, F and C, which may reflect the existence of scale economies in production. Finally, the exchange rate had a positive effect on the small-car prices of F and C (significant at the 10% level).

2. Medium-Sized Domestic Cars

a. Domestic Intermediate Car Quantity Equations. The results of the output regressions for medium-sized cars built by U.S. based assemblers are shown in Table 4. Among the "big three" producers in the U.S., the direct effect of the VRAs on output was statistically insignificant in all cases except for the initial effect on Ford, which was large, negative (-.39) and significant at the 20% level. It is surprising that the effects of the VRAs on output were not negative for all domestic intermediate models, particularly in the long-run. Feenstra (1984, 1985a and 1985b) has shown that one of the major effects of the VRAs was to create incentives for Japanese firms to increase their sales of larger cars with higher unit profitability in the U.S. market, in response to numerical quota limits, which might be expected to suppress sales of domestic intermediate models. On the other hand, to the extent that the VRAs raised import prices, it is reasonable to assume that there would have been substitution from expensive imports to domestic intermediates. The

TABLE 4

INTERMEDIATE CAR QUANTITY ESTIMATES

Dependent Variable:	LOGQMGM	LOGQMF	LOGQMC	LOGQMAM
Independent Variable:	Estimated Coefficient	Estimated Coefficient	Estimated Coefficient	Estimated Coefficient
C	-21.992	-45.810	38.687	2.640
	(-1.211)	(-1.939)	(-1.293)	(0.525)
LOGPIMP	-0.440	-0.445	-2.317	3.252
	(-0.928)	(-0.753)	(-2.480)	(2.910)
LGPBRMyy	-0.246	2.204	-0.033	-4.692
	(-0.292)	(1.849)	(-0.025)	(-1.817)
LOGGNP8	5.567	4.736	5.915	-2.083
	(2.470)	(1.686)	(1.519)	(-0.364)
LOGGASP8	0.282	-0.718	-0.722	-0.764
	(0.676)	(-1.385)	(-0.965)	(-0.564)
REALR	-0.027	0.047	-0.197	0.005
	(-1.014)	(1.432)	(-4.209)	(0.082)
TIME	-0.026	-0.043	0.020	-0.123
	(-1.456)	(-1.901)	(0.606)	(-2.674)
VRA	0.137	-0.389	0.149	1.276
	(0.773)	(-1.602)	(0.490)	(2.863)
VRA1	-0.068	0.068	-0.233	0.883
	(-0.343)	(0.284)	(-0.543)	(1.496)
G1	0.369	1.374	0.281	0.644
	(1.266)	(3.784)	(0.533)	(0.966)
G2	-0.193	-0.487	-1.462	3.672
	(-0.771)	(-1.574)	(-3.046)	(4.973)
LOGUAWC8	-0.045	-1.587	1.733	4.796
	(-0.035)	(-0.976)	(0.777)	(1.170)
LOGCAPU	-0.158	0.667	2.603	-0.528
	(-0.206)	(0.670)	(1.590)	(-0.265)
REALWGM	-0.643	1.967	0.166	-1.596
	(-0.744)	(-1.865)	(0.098)	(-0.752)
REALWF	-0.668	2.102	-2.002	5.943
	(-0.446)	(1.132)	(-0.665)	(1.674)
REALWC	0.689	1.046	2.594	-4.669
	(0.805)	(0.983)	(1.606)	(-2.404)
REALRGM	2.162	1.058	-4.494	3.450
	(1.431)	(0.568)	(-1.467)	(0.937)
REALRF	7.968	14.537	34.871	4.188
	(1.477)	(2.168)	(3.152)	(0.341)
REALRC	-5.374	-12.496	-17.186	-5.770
	(-1.459)	(-2.718)	(-2.306)	(-0.667)
LOGEXRJ	-0.041	0.483	0.898	1.348
	(-0.106)	(1.014)	(1.277)	(1.428)
Q1DUM				-0.571
				(-2.577)
Q2DUM				-0.529
				(-2.869)
Q3DUM				-0.576
				(-2.793)
ADJUSTED R-SQUARED =	0.588	0.870	0.900	0.897
DURBIN-WATSON STATISTIC =	2.014	2.02	1.923	
F-STATISTIC = (19, 42) =	5.582	22.577	30.018	22.341
FINAL VALUE RHO =				.574
T-STATISTIC RHO =				4.641

results for large cars (section 3, below) suggest that the VRAs may have had their most significant quantity effects (from Japanese quality upgrading) in the large car market, perhaps in conjunction with the effects of fuel economy regulations, after the import restraints had been in effect for a few years.

The effect of the VRAs on Ford's intermediate output reflects strategic choices Ford made during the 1980s. Ford's Taurus/Sable line (an intermediate sized car) was introduced in 1986 and widely touted in the industry and business press as a major technological advance for Ford. However the Taurus/Sable line replaced an older, lower priced set of models, in much the same way that Japanese producers upgraded the quality and cost of their U.S. exports under the VRAs. The introduction of the Taurus series was undoubtedly a major contributor to the dramatic growth in profits which Ford experienced in 1986 and 1987.[20] It may also have led to a *reduction* in the number of intermediate-sized cars produced by Ford. When introduced in 1986, the median base (wholesale) price of a Taurus was $9,750, as compared with a 1985 median price of $7,970 for the downsized LTD-'83 that it replaced in the Ford line. Sales of the Taurus for the first 9 months of 86 were only 2% greater than sales of the LTD-'83 for the same period in 85, in spite of the tremendous amount of interest generated by the car's introduction (total U.S. intermediate sales rose 3% in the same period).

Ford's sales of medium-size cars were most directly affected by the quality upgrading response of Japanese producers in response to the VRAs. In response, Ford brought out a new line of higher-priced cars to meet the Japanese competitive challenge in the intermediate market segments. Absent the VRAs, it is unlikely that new intermediate offerings from Ford would have been so expensive. On the other hand, the VRAs may have accelerated the pace of innovation in car design at Ford.

The results for the coefficient for the average price of other domestic cars (LGPBRMyy) are mixed, both in sign and in significance. While it remains true that domestic firms raise their prices when average domestic prices of other cars go up, as shown in the next section, the effects of changes in LGPBRMyy on output are different from those found for small cars. This is at least partly explained by the fact that intermediate prices are not as closely correlated with the LGPBRxyy variable as were small car prices, especially for Ford, as shown in Table 5. Increases in average prices (LGPBRMyy) increased output for Ford and reduced it for AM (both significant at the 10%

level), and had no significant effect on intermediate output for either
GM or Chrysler.

TABLE 5

**SIMPLE CORRELATION COEFFICIENTS BETWEEN
LOGPxyy and LGPBRxyy, BY FIRM AND SIZE CLASS**

Size Class\Firm:	GM	Ford	Chrys	AM	4-Firm Average
Small	.96	.96	.89	.92	.93
Medium	.97	.87	.95	.87	.92
Large	.98	.92	.79	.-	.89

Import prices had no significant effect on intermediate output for
F and GM, had a large negative effect on Chrysler output and a large
positive effect on AM output. This suggests that Chrysler and AM's
intermediate products were closer substitutes for imports than were GM
and Ford cars.

Changes in the level of national income had large and significant
effects on the sales of intermediate cars, as was the case with small
cars. As durable commodities, vehicles have generally been found to
have strongly pro-cyclical output patterns, which is confirmed in these
results. Real interest rates had negative and strongly significant effects
only on the output level of Chrysler intermediates. This could represent
a supply-side effect, to the extent that Chrysler had trouble raising
capital for expansion when interest rates were high, due to its financial
difficulties. Such problems at Chrysler could also explain the positive
effect (weakly significant) of interest rates on Ford output, if potential
Chrysler customers were diverted to Ford when interest rates were high.
The time trend is negative, and significant at at least the 20% level for
3 out of the four firms, suggesting a long-run decline in the sales of
domestic intermediates of 2-4% per year, for Ford and GM, reflecting
changes in tastes due to both higher gasoline prices and increasing
consumer preferences for imported cars.

The price of gasoline had a (weakly) significant direct effect only
for Ford intermediates. However, the two gasoline crises of the 1980s
did apparently produce some substantial demand shifts. Output of
intermediates rose significantly for Ford, and to a lesser extent for the
other domestic producers, after the first gasoline crisis (G1). This
represents a shift of demand from large to intermediate-size cars.
However, by 1979 the shift from intermediates to small cars and
imports dominates. The effect of the second gas crisis was generally
negative and was statistically significant at the 10% level for Ford and
Chrysler intermediate sales.

Own firm-specific wage rates do not have the expected negative effect on the output of intermediate cars for Ford and Chrysler. This may be a result of the failure of competitive mechanisms in the labor market. If wages are more likely to rise when output is high, then there will be a positive correlation between wage rates and the level of output, exactly the opposite of what would be predicted by the theory of competitive labor markets. Again, this suggests that the association between labor costs and output should be viewed as a simple correlation, and not the usual direct cause and effect relationship. However, these results are not strongly significant and other explanations for these results are available.[21]

The coefficients for real firm-specific capital costs (REALRyy) for Ford and GM are generally positive and significant for the firm output equations, and negative and significant for Chrysler capital costs, reflecting the latter's competitive problems in the late 70s and early 80s. The capacity utilization term (LOGCAPU) was significant only for Chrysler, suggesting that the larger firms may have exhausted scale economies in the intermediate product segments. The effect of the Japanese exchange rate is insignificant for all firms in this size group, suggesting again that intermediate cars are not close substitutes for imports.

b. Domestic Intermediate Car Price Equations. The results of the price regressions for medium-sized cars built by U.S. based assemblers are shown in Table 6, which reveals a major difference in the competitive strategies of the major U.S. auto producers, under the VRAs. Simply put, GM's prices increased about 10%, Ford's prices fell about 20% and Chrysler's prices were basically unchanged as a result of the VRAs.[22] The results for GM and Ford are strongly significant for the initial effect (VRA). In the long-run, the VRAs led to a further increase of about 4% in GM prices (significant at the 20% level) and insignificant price changes for the other producers.

Changes in the average prices of other cars had a positive effect on medium-sized car prices for GM, F and C, which was significant at the 5% level. The coefficients are all positive, and for F and C are much larger in magnitude than were the coefficients on LGPBRxyy for small cars. The t-statistics are higher for LGPBRxyy for the intermediate sized cars than they were for the small cars. These results suggest that the level of market power and the degree of pricing awareness and coordination is much higher in the medium-car segment than it is in the small-car portion of the market. There is some evidence that GM is functioning as a price leader in this market segment. Simple plotting of the price trends, done in chapter IV, suggests that smaller firms tend to

TABLE 6

INTERMEDIATE CAR PRICE ESTIMATES

Dependent Variable:	LOGPMGM	LOGPMF	LOGPMC	LOGPMAN
Independent Variable:	Estimated Coefficient	Estimated Coefficient	Estimated Coefficient	Estimated Coefficient
C	5.433	-2.312	2.929	-2.323
	(2.410)	(-0.414)	(0.616)	(-0.434)
LOGPIMP	0.063	-0.017	-0.241	-0.164
	(1.079)	(-0.115)	(-1.979)	(-1.183)
LGPBRMyy	0.303	0.663	0.545	-0.086
	(2.892)	(2.346)	(2.505)	(-0.268)
LOGGNP8	0.243	0.833	0.910	0.171
	(0.869)	(1.216)	(1.564)	(0.240)
LOGGASP8	0.004	-0.105	-0.144	-0.029
	(0.070)	(-0.821)	(-1.358)	(-0.171)
REALR	0.000	0.004	0.005	0.005
	(0.097)	(0.539)	(0.674)	(0.677)
TIME	-0.000	0.002	0.003	-0.005
	(-0.048)	(0.349)	(0.566)	(-0.947)
VRA	0.102	-0.195	0.006	-0.170
	(4.646)	(3.278)	(0.125)	(-3.073)
VRA1	0.040	0.007	0.061	0.097
	(1.642)	(0.104)	(1.218)	(1.330)
G1	-0.016	0.054	0.054	-0.168
	(-0.430)	(0.598)	(0.713)	(-2.032)
G2	0.072	-0.077	0.021	0.402
	(2.330)	(-0.968)	(0.316)	(4.389)
LOGUAWC8	0.106	0.410	-0.254	0.554
	(0.654)	(1.034)	(-0.759)	(1.088)
LOGCAPU	-0.320	-0.034	-0.943	-0.081
	(-3.351)	(-0.128)	(-4.922)	(-0.329)
REALWGM	-0.083	0.175	0.055	0.510
	(-0.776)	(0.650)	(0.237)	(1.935)
REALWF	0.061	-1.023	0.053	0.412
	(0.325)	(-2.117)	(0.137)	(0.936)
REALWC	-0.231	0.317	-0.010	-0.279
	(-2.173)	(1.185)	(-0.047)	(-1.160)
REALRGM	0.601	-0.331	-0.361	-0.452
	(3.206)	(-0.674)	(-0.929)	(-0.989)
REALRF	-1.615	-0.052	0.137	-2.583
	(-2.412)	(-0.030)	(0.099)	(-1.693)
REALRC	1.243	-1.017	-0.777	2.600
	(2.720)	(-0.859)	(-0.818)	(2.423)
LOGEXRJ	-0.001	-0.073	0.039	-0.053
	(-0.014)	(-0.61	(0.393)	(-0.456)
Q1DUM				-0.047
				(-1.693)
Q2DUM				-0.026
				(-1.123)
Q3DUM				-0.005
				(-0.206)
ADJUSTED R-SQUARED =	0.988	0.977	0.977	0.917
DURBIN-WATSON STATISTIC =	1.867	1.897	1.837	
F-STATISTIC (19, 42) =	269.940	129.804	138.225	27.999
FINAL VALUE RHO =		.228		
T-STATISTIC RHO =		1.501		

follow GM price increases, with a lag of at least one year. The fact that the coefficient for LGPBRxyy rises in inverse proportion to market share in the medium-sized market suggests that the smaller firms follow market prices more closely than does GM. This relationship may have begun to break down during the VRAs, as foreign competition increased in the medium-sized car market, as suggested by the effect of the VRAs on Ford output and price levels. Import prices had a significant, negative, effect only on Chrysler's prices.

Macroeconomic variables generally did not have significant effects on the prices of intermediate-sized cars. The only exception to this pattern is a (weakly significant) tendency for Chrysler prices to rise with national output (LOGGNP8), and for AM prices to fall with national output. There was no significant time trend, nor any tendency for prices to respond to changes in the real interest rate. These observations are surprising, given the strong relationship between intermediate car *output* and gnp. This finding again reflects the extent of market power and pricing coordination among domestic producers. Price wars during downturns, of the type found by Bresnahan (1981a) in the 1950s aren't of sufficient frequency or duration to be detected in this study.[23]

A similar result was obtained for the effects of changes in gasoline prices on intermediate car prices. Again the effects are not statistically significant in most cases. The most important exception is the effect of the 2nd gas shock (G2) on GM intermediate prices, which was positive and significant at the 5% level. GM's sales of medium-sized cars were not reduced by the second gas crisis, as was the case for Ford and Chrysler (Table 4). GM apparently used the second gas crisis to raise the price of its intermediate-sized cars, rather than output. Chrysler had a weak tendency to lower its intermediate car prices when gasoline prices rose, reflecting the lower fuel efficiencies of its products. AM's prices tended to fall after the second gas crisis, but this may have been the result of AM's general competitive difficulties in the late 1970s.

Factor costs again have an unexpected effect on prices. Own wage rates and capital costs generally tend to have a negative effect on a firm's prices in these equations. The major exception to this pattern is the effect of GM's capital costs on its own prices, which is positive and significant at the 1% level.

The industry-wide level of capacity utilization (LOGCAPU) has a large, negative and very significant effect on prices for GM, C and AM medium sized cars. This simply reflects downward sloping demand curves. In order to sell more cars and increase capacity utilization, prices have to fall (*ceteris paribus*). The same general result was obtained in the small-car price equations. The Yen/Dollar exchange rate had no significant effects on prices for any of the domestic firms, confirming the observation that prior to the VRAs import competition was not an important factor in the intermediate market.

3. Large-sized Domestic Cars

a. Domestic Large Car Quantity Equations. The results of the output regressions for large cars built by U.S.-based assemblers are shown in Table 7. The initial direct effects of the VRAs were mixed, with a negative effect on GM output (significant at the 10% level), a positive effect on Ford (insignificant) and negative effect on Chrysler (insignificant). However, after three years under the VRAs, the effect for all three firms (VRA1) is large, negative and statistically significant at at least the 10% confidence level. These negative direct effects on the output of large cars are larger than those for other size classes (in percentage terms), far surpassing any positive effects of the VRAs on the small car segments in terms of the numbers of units sold. These large-car output effects are at least partially the result of quality upgrading on the part of Japanese firms, in response to the VRAs. However, they also reflect strategic decisions by domestic firms to set much higher prices for domestically-designed large cars, with the concomitant loss of unit sales in this market segment, as shown in the next section.

One caveat which must be noted in interpreting the results for the effects of the VRAs on domestic large car sales is that the dummy variable VRA1 may also be picking up changes in model designs and prices which were induced by the CAFE standards and gas guzzler taxes. The CAFE standards rose to 27.5 mpg in 1985, resulting in penalties for both GM and Ford, as noted above. In 1986 the Dept. of Transportation relaxed the CAFE standard to 26 mpg, where it will remain through 1989.

The gas guzzler excise tax constituted a further incentive to downsize or eliminate large-sized cars. According to Henderson (1985) the threat of this tax resulted in 1) a decline in the average engine size of a large car from 312 cubic inches in 1980 to 297 in 1984; and 2) GM consideration of a plan to classify a new large station wagon as a truck (treated under a separate, more lenient, CAFE standard).[24] These standards regulations clearly influenced the design, cost and optimal model mix of each of the domestic manufacturers in the 1984-1986 period. Because it takes several years to design and market new car models, the responses of the U.S.-based auto assemblers to impending penalties under the fuel economy regulations were already being put

TABLE 7

LARGE CAR QUANTITY ESTIMATES

Dependent Variable:	LOGQLGM	LOGQLF	LOGQLC
Independent Variable:	Estimated Coefficient	Estimated Coefficient	Estimated Coefficient
C	-23.325	-11.176	-23.323
	(-1.608)	(-0.408)	(-0.599)
LOGPIMP	-0.954	-1.194	-0.046
	(-2.908)	(-1.587)	(-0.044)
LGPBRLyy	1.697	0.204	2.239
	(2.155)	(0.144)	(1.315)
LOGGNP8	1.885	1.029	0.053
	(1.162)	(0.306)	(0.010)
LOGGASP8	-0.455	0.356	0.432
	(-1.523)	(0.561)	(0.443)
REALR	0.147	-0.093	-0.052
	(0.784)	(-2.341)	(-0.849)
TIME	-0.796	0.015	-0.073
	(-0.627)	(0.556)	(-1.894)
VRA	-0.258	0.147	-0.279
	(-1.781)	(0.524)	(-0.711)
VRA1	-0.590	-0.573	-1.023
	(-4.780)	(-1.725)	(-2.442)
G1	-0.157	-0.240	0.810
	(-0.760)	(-0.541)	(1.231)
G2	-0.402	-0.594	0.065
	(-2.357)	(-1.494)	(0.116)
LOGUAWC8	0.940	-1.205	7.890
	(1.004)	(-0.624)	(2.688)
LOGCAPU	2.204	2.828	4.633
	(3.988)	(2.124)	(2.448)
REALWGM	1.041	1.848	-1.597
	(1.764)	(1.360)	(-0.861)
REALWF	-1.572	-0.245	-8.113
	(-1.540)	(-0.101)	(-2.402)
REALWC	1.254	1.393	2.821
	(2.085)	(1.051)	(1.446)
REALRGM	-1.691	-4.840	8.831
	(-1.687)	(-1.961)	(2.613)
REALRF	9.577	24.584	26.966
	(2.625)	(2.785)	(2.187)
REALRC	-4.581	-5.221	-24.739
	(-1.789)	(-0.881)	(-2.952)
LOGEXRJ	0.124	0.876	-0.647
	(0.459)	(1.491)	(-0.748)
ADJUSTED R-SQUARED =	0.964	0.914	0.926
DURBIN-WATSON STATISTIC =	2.081	1.790	1.864
F-STATISTIC (19, 42) =	85.633	35.149	41.137
FINAL VALUE RHO =	-0.215	0.303	
T-STATISTIC RHO =	-1.433	2.094	

into effect when the CAFE standards were relaxed. Crandall, Gruenspect, Keeler and Lave (1986) point out that the CAFE standards may have had the unintentional effect of reducing the competitiveness of domestic auto manufacturers. The results presented here support that hypothesis. Thus is would not be correct to assign all of the output reduction associated with the VRA1 variable to the VRAs. This issue will be addressed in Chapter VI, where the model is used to estimate price and output in the absence of the VRAs.

Increases in the prices of other cars had a positive and significant effect on GM and C output. This result reflects the expected substitution effect, which was not found consistently with either small or medium output equations. The correlation between LGPBRLyy and own prices was lowest for large cars, as shown in Table 5 above, which explains why substitution effects are identified in this market segment.

Import prices, on the other hand, had large, negative and significant effects on the output of large cars. The effect is probably negative because the movement of Japanese-based firms into the production of larger, more expensive cars apparently displaced some of the output of domestic large-car makers.

The macroeconomic variables, LOGGNP8 and REALR generally had insignificant effects on large-car output, the only exception being a large, negative and significant coefficient on the real interest rate for Ford. Large car demand is generally somewhat less sensitive to income levels than is the demand for other vehicle classes, because fluctuations in GNP tend to have a smaller effect on the high-income segments of the population. The time trend is significant only for Chrysler, reflecting its general competitive difficulties. Thus the secular decline in large car output is a recent phenomena, coincident with the period of the VRAs and the implementation of the CAFE standards and gas guzzler tax.

Gasoline prices had a significant negative effect on the output of GM cars, both directly through the LOGGASP8 variable and through the shift variable G2. The negative effect on Ford was somewhat smaller and less significant, showing up only in the G2 shift variable. The gas crises had no detectable effect on Chrysler, with all fuel cost variables having positive and insignificant coefficients in its equation. These results reflect differences in firm structure and strategies with respect to fuel economy regulations. GM has historically had the highest proportion of large car sales among the domestic producers with smaller proportions for Ford and Chrysler. Thus higher gas prices and the fuel economy regulations could be expected to have their largest effects on GM, and then Ford and have the smallest effect on Chrysler.[25] This ordering was reinforced by a Chrysler decision in one year (1981) to dramatically reorganize its product lines, downsizing and eliminating several larger model lines in order to improve fleet fuel economy (Henderson, 1985).[26]

Own firm-specific wage rates do not have the expected negative effect on the output of large cars for GM and Chrysler, and the negative coefficient for Ford is insignificant, providing some support for the contention that the auto industry labor market is not competitively structured. The coefficients for real firm-specific capital costs (REALRyy) are mixed, but generally strongly significant. The capacity utilization term (LOGCAPU) was significant and positive for all three firms, reflecting business cycle factors again. The effect of the Yen/Dollar exchange rate is insignificant for all firms in this size group, suggesting again that intermediate cars are not viewed by the public as close substitutes for imports.

b. Domestic Large Car Price Equations. The results of the price regressions for large cars built by U.S. based assemblers are shown in Table 8, which reveals another difference in the competitive strategies of Ford and GM under the VRAs and fuel economy regulations in effect in the early 1980s. GM *reduced* prices by about 5%, while Ford raised prices about 20% on its large cars in the later stages of the VRA. These results are weakly significant for the VRA1 variable. There were no other statistically significant *direct* effects of the VRAs on large car prices.

To the extent that the VRAs raised *average* car prices in the U.S., they resulted in an *indirect* increase in large car prices because the coefficient for LGPBRLyy is positive and significant (at least the 20% level) for all domestic assemblers. Indirect effects are examined in Chapter VI, below. LOGPIMP had an insignificant effect on the prices of all three producers, as expected. GNP had no significant effect either, reflecting the stability of large car demand, with respect to business cycle fluctuations. The TIME trend was only weakly significant for Ford and GM, and the coefficients were also quite small. Neither real interest rates and nor gasoline prices were important in explaining large car priced movements.

Cost factors do play some role in explaining price movements for large cars. Capacity utilization has a negative effect on prices (significant at the 10% level for GM) for all three domestic producers, as it did for intermediate cars. UAW labor costs, own labor costs and GM capital cost all had statistically significant effects on Ford Prices. Only UAW labor costs and exchange rates had significant effects on Chrysler prices, but the sign for the labor costs was incorrect. Thus large car prices are largely determined in this model by strategic interactions (through the LGPBRLyy variable) and by factor costs. The

TABLE 8

LARGE CAR PRICE ESTIMATES

Dependent Variable:	LOGPLGM	LOGPLF	LOGPLC
Independent Variable	Estimated Coefficient	Estimated Coefficient	Estimated Coefficient
C	1.147	-4.446	14.618
	(0.343)	(-0.417)	(2.310)
LOGPIMP	-0.039	0.412	-0.133
	(-0.487)	(1.250)	(-0.613)
LGPBRLyy	0.658	0.924	0.335
	(3.531)	(1.697)	(1.307)
LOGGNP8	0.376	1.042	-0.573
	(0.984)	(0.773)	(-0.674)
LOGGASP8	0.102	-0.279	0.131
	(1.431)	(-1.061)	(0.769)
REALR	-0.004	0.025	0.005
	(-0.942)	(1.541)	(0.457)
TIME	0.004	-0.016	0.001
	(1.452)	(-1.380)	(0.193)
VRA	0.031	0.035	0.054
	(0.900)	(0.321)	(0.862)
VRA1	-0.051	0.204	-0.073
	(-1.620)	(1.332)	(-0.714)
G1	-0.096	0.158	0.105
	(-1.949)	(0.870)	(0.917)
G2	-0.019	0.077	0.067
	(-0.444)	(0.459)	(0.632)
LOGUAWC8	-0.079	1.351	-0.825
	(-0.354)	(1.800)	(-1.843)
LOGCAPU	-0.275	-0.592	-0.281
	(-1.977)	(-1.001)	(-0.745)
REALRGM	-0.231	2.490	-0.264
	(-0.914)	(2.337)	(-0.386)
REALRF	0.198	-4.542	0.907
	(0.217)	(-1.161)	(0.356)
REALRC	0.623	-1.205	0.157
	(0.996)	(-0.461)	(0.095)
LOGEXRJ	0.064	-0.274	-0.238
	(0.988)	(-1.123)	(-1.523)
ADJUSTED R-SQUARED =	0.986	0.972	0.988
DURBIN-WATSON STATISTIC =	2.033	1.290	1.953
F-STATISTIC (19, 42) =	231.906	111.681	261.307
FINAL VALUE RHO =		.650	.818
T-STATISTIC RHO =		5.728	9.661

VRAs and the fuel economy regulations apparently produced some shifts in the nature of the competitive pricing strategies of U.S. large car makers.

4. Imported Cars

The results of the output and price regressions for imported cars are reported in Table 9. The direct effect of the VRAs was to reduce output and raise the prices of imported cars. In the short-run, this effect was significant at the 2% level for output and at the 1% level for prices. In the long-run, there was an additional direct reduction in imports caused by the VRAs (weakly significant), despite the relaxation of the quota and the introduction of new imports from Korea into the U.S. market. The price effect of the VRAs was reduced but not eliminated in the long-run (VRA1 is negative), confirming the hypothesis that the VRAs continued to constitute a significant constraint on imports after 1984.

These direct effects were offset somewhat by price/substitution effects. Changes in the average price of domestic cars (LOGPBUS) were positively correlated with import sales, although this effect was not significant at even the 20% level. It is interesting that average domestic prices had no significant effect on the *prices* of imports, suggesting that competition *among* imports was a more important determinant of pricing behavior than was the pricing behavior of domestic manufacturers. In aggregate, the import market appears to have been much more competitive than the market for domestic cars, at least in terms of its responsiveness to average domestic prices.

GNP had the expected positive effect on import quantity and prices. The TIME trend had no significant effect on the overall quantity of imports, suggesting that the growth of imports over this time period can be explained by, or is at least correlated with, the other variables included in this model. The TIME trend has a weak negative effect on import prices, which is explained by the rising share of low-cost Japanese vehicles in the import mix in the 1970s. Real interest rates have a strong, significant and negative effect on output and no significant effect on import prices.

The effects of higher gasoline prices are captured by the dummy variables G1 and G2. The first gasoline crisis, which was associated with a major U.S. recession, the decline in European imports and the growth of Japanese imports combined to produced a negative effect on the total number of imports. After the 1979 gas crisis the shift to Japanese imports was more pronounced and U.S. income remained stable. As a result, the effect of G2 is positive and significant. If this

TABLE 9

IMPORT CAR PRICE AND QUANTITY ESTIMATES

Dependent Variable:	LOGQIMP	LOGPIMP
Dependent Variable	Estimated Coefficient	Estimated Coefficient
C	-20.403	4.790
	(-1.774)	(1.623)
LOGPBUS	0.634	-0.027
	(1.282)	(-0.232)
LOGGNP8	2.259	0.581
	(1.679)	(1.487)
LOGGASP8	0.209	0.019
	(0.875)	(0.257)
REALR	-0.046	-0.003
	(-2.792)	(-0.727)
TIME	0.012	-0.006
	(1.039)	(-1.588)
VRA	-0.344	0.353
	(-2.647)	(8.255)
VRA1	-0.151	-0.106
	(-1.506)	(-2.518)
G1	-1.143	0.592
	(-5.521)	(7.300)
G2	0.506	-0.409
	(3.076)	(-7.673)
LOGUAWC8	2.625	-1.962
	(2.965)	(-7.086)
LOGCAPU	-0.325	-0.193
	(-0.763)	(-1.162)
REALWGM	1.306	-0.925
	(2.442)	(-4.449)
REALWF	0.118	0.988
	(0.147)	(3.324)
REALWC	-2.264	1.777
	(-3.354)	(7.924)
REALRGM	-1.991	-1.053
	(-2.510)	(-3.743)
REALRF	-2.581	9.469
	(-0.866)	(8.506)
REALRC	8.682	-7.803
	(3.832)	(-8.084)
LOGEXRJ	-0.001	-0.068
	(-0.003)	(-0.997)
ADJUSTED R-SQUARED =	0.951	.997
DURBIN-WATSON STATISTIC =	2.057	1.794
F-STATISTIC (18, 43) =	67.438	1123.830
FINAL VALUE RHO =	-0.221	0.651
T-STATISTIC RHO =	-1.482	5.864

regression were for Japanese auto imports only, the sign of G1 would probably also be positive. It is interesting to note that real import prices rose after the first gas crisis and fell after the second crisis.[27]

As UAW wages and firm specific labor costs for GM rose in the 1970s, auto imports increased and the prices of imports fell. Other factor costs also had significant effects on auto imports and prices, but no consistent patterns are revealed in these results. Surprisingly, changes in exchange rates had no significant effects on either the prices or the output of imports. Two factors contribute to this result. First, the dummy variables VRA and VRA1 explain more of the increase in import prices which occurred in the early 1980s, the most significant period of dollar appreciation in these regressions. Second, Japanese producers were experiencing rapid productivity growth during the 1976-1978 period when the dollar was appreciating, as reflected in the MCD, which offset the effects of adverse exchange rate movements on Japanese auto prices.

5. Factor Cost Equations

a. Wage Regressions. The results in Table 10 show that the VRAs affected the average hourly cost of UAW labor and the average compensation of employees of each of the big three firms in quite different ways. The VRAs did not have a statistically significant effect on the total compensation received by UAW members. Real hourly labor costs for unionized employees did increase significantly during the 1970s because of the effects of higher gasoline prices and the gas crises in 1974 and 1979. Since the majority of hourly employees for each of the big three firms are covered by UAW contracts the differences in the effects of the VRAs on labor cost at the firm level in the firm-specific labor cost regressions reflect changes in the compensation of other employees (principally management personnel and employees located abroad), and changes in the share of managerial employees in the labor force.[28]

The VRAs resulted in an increase in real labor costs at GM, and a fall in real labor costs at Ford and Chrysler. The timing and magnitude of the changes differ across firms, as well. Ford's labor costs fall during the early stages of the VRAs by about 3.5% (the VRA effect, which is weakly significant), then remain unchanged at that level in the long-run (no significant VRA1 effect). Chrysler's labor costs fall about 14% initially (strongly significant), and then rebound by about +7% in the long-run. The initiation of the VRAs does not result in any significant change in GM's labor costs. However, GM's labor costs rise by about 13% in the long-run. This result for GM is surprising, in view of the

TABLE 10

UAW AND FIRM-SPECIFIC LABOR COST ESTIMATES

Dependent Variable:	REALWGM	REALWF	REALWC	LOGUAWC8
Independent Variable:	Estimated Coefficient	Estimated Coefficient	Estimated Coefficient	Estimated Coefficient
C	-21.664	-10.705	-6.39	1.215
	(-7.217)	(-6.222)	(-2.664)	(0.535)
LOGGNP8	3.184	1.420	0.878	0.452
	(7.471)	(5.816)	(2.484)	(1.425)
LOGGASP8	-0.301	-0.137	0.050	0.118
	(-4.269)	(-3.414)	(0.869)	(2.285)
REALR	-0.007	-0.008	0.001	0.003
	(-1.162)	(-2.414)	(0.122)	(0.777)
TIME	-0.021	-0.006	-0.002	-0.001
	(-5.743)	(-2.850)	(-0.614)	(-0.446)
VRA	0.020	-0.034	-0.143	0.005
	(0.507)	(-1.588)	(-5.162)	(0.173)
VRA1	0.128	-0.009	0.071	-0.010
	(4.143)	(-0.512)	(2.772)	(-0.429)
G1	0.109	-0.051	-0.203	0.061
	(2.797)	(-2.304)	(-6.390)	(2.195)
G2	0.013	-0.030	0.193	0.027
	(0.374)	(-1.478)	(6.983)	(1.008)
LOGUAWC8	0.262	0.896	1.326	
	(1.559)	(9.697)	(11.951)	
LOGCAPU	-0.496	-0.007	-0.040	-0.332
	(-2.502)	(-0.064)	(-0.250)	(-2.310)
LOGEXRJ	0.303	0.095	-0.112	-0.096
	(3.610)	(1.970)	(-1.596)	(-1.569)
ADJUSTED R-SQUARED =	0.886	0.963	0.978	0.928
DURBIN-WATSON STATISTIC =	1.933	1.921	1.868	1.965
F-STATISTIC (11, 50) =	44.026	139.106	251.791	79.455
FINAL VALUE RHO =	0.219	0.287	0.562	0.039
T-STATISTIC RHO =	1.578	2.108	4.939	0.283

fact that the VRA had a weak tendency to *reduce* the cost of capital (and hence stockholders return on equity) in the later half of the VRA experience, as shown below.

The results for GM are particularly significant in view of the fact that total profits at GM peaked in 1985 yet profits continued to rise at Ford through 1987 (see note 20, this chapter). This result suggests the possibility of principal-agent problems and raises questions about the efficiency of corporate governance within GM because the profit-gap between GM and Ford may be partially explained by differences in management compensation (including bonuses and stock options) in the two firms.

The effect of UAW labor costs on firm-specific labor costs declines with firm-size, both in size of the effect and in significance levels. This is surprising, in view of the fact that the level of vertical integration-- and hence the degree of reliance on unionized labor in the production process--increases with firm size. This result provides further detail to the observation by Flynn that white collar wage differences are an important determinant of the MCD. The implication of these results is that white collar labor cost problems, vis-a-vis Japanese production cost patterns, are most severe at GM and decline with firm size.

It is also interesting to note that labor costs rise most strongly and significantly with the Japanese exchange rate at GM, with a smaller positive response at Ford and a negative response at Chrysler and for all UAW labor. Increases in the exchange rate raise the delivered cost of Japanese vehicles in the U.S., providing opportunities for domestic manufacturers to raise prices, and returns to labor. A similar pattern of results was obtained for the LOGGNP8 variable. GM is apparently maximizing returns to non-union labor, in contrast to the traditional model of the profit maximizing firm. GM's managers may be engaging in satisfying behavior. This hypothesis is an important topic for future research.

b. Firm-Specific Capital Cost Regressions. The results in Table 11 show that the VRAs led to an increase in capital costs (and hence profits) at Ford and had no significant effect on capital costs at GM and Chrysler. The failure of capital costs to rise at GM reflects its loss of competitiveness in this 1980s, as disclosed in its loss of market share in this period. It may also be a result of the labor cost changes described above. The effects on Ford's capital costs are small, relative to the effects of the VRAs on its labor costs. Capital costs at Ford increase by about 1% initially, and by an additional 1% in the long-run (both effects significant at the 10% level).

Gasoline prices and the gas crises reduced capital costs at all three firms. The effect of gas prices was largest for GM, and smallest for Chrysler. Both G1 and G2 had negative effects on GM's capital cost (significant at the 5% level), but Ford was unaffected by the first gas crisis and capital costs at Chrysler increased after G1. Chrysler was less affected by gasoline-cost factors than the other U.S. producers because of its long-standing captive import arrangements with Mitsubishi Motors. No other variables had significant effects on capital costs across all three firms.

TABLE 11

FIRM-SPECIFIC CAPITAL COST ESTIMATES

Dependent Variable:	REALRGM	REALRF	REALRC
Dependent Variable	Estimated Coefficient	Estimated Coefficient	Estimated Coefficient
C	-3.574	0.094	-0.237
	(-2.021)	(0.171)	(-0.288)
LOGGNP8	0.479	-0.001	-0.013
	(1.904)	(-0.008)	(-0.110)
LOGGASP8	-0.114	-0.070	-0.043
	(-2.683)	(-5.314)	(-2.139)
REALR	0.001	0.002	0.002
	(0.292)	(2.559)	(1.685)
TIME	-0.001	0.000	0.001
	(-0.607)	(0.091)	(0.557)
VRA	0.000	0.010	0.010
	(0.028)	(1.959)	(1.224)
VRA1	-0.017	0.010	-0.001
	(-1.034)	(1.945)	(-0.079)
G1	-0.050	0.001	0.024
	(-2.362)	(0.086)	(2.446)
G2	-0.048	-0.010	-0.018
	(-2.706)	(-1.790)	(-2.246)
LOGUAWC8	-0.023	-0.016	0.047
	(-0.364)	(-0.825)	(1.601)
LOGCAPU	-0.066	-0.021	0.017
	(-0.611)	(-0.612)	(0.329)
LOGEXRJ	0.051	0.010	0.020
	(1.054)	(0.643)	(0.884)
ADJUSTED R SQUARED =	0.415	0.527	0.291
DURBIN-WATSON STATISTIC =	1.805	1.544	1.904
F-STATISTIC (11, 50) =	4.913	7.169	3.268
FINAL VALUE RHO =	0.815	0.820	0.830
T-STATISTIC RHO =	10.309	11.032	10.901

TABLE 12

LONG-RUN PRICE EFFECTS OF THE VRAS, BY FIRM AND SIZE CLASS

Size Class/Firm	GM	Ford	Chrysler	AM
Small Cars	+.052	+.237	+.20	-.013
Intermediate Cars	+.142	-.188	+.067	-.073
Large Cars	-.020	+.239	-.019	
Simple Average	+.058	+.096	+.083	-.043

D. Firm-level Results

Chapter VI will use the model estimated above to analyze the direct and indirect effects of the VRAs and fuel economy regulations on output, prices and employment in the domestic auto industry. Overall, the direct effects identified in this chapter show that GM suffered large losses in total output (over the three size classes) in the long-run, Ford somewhat smaller output losses and Chrysler gained output as a result of these policies. The price effects, and the estimated responses of the domestic firms to changes in the prices of other firms, suggest that there were large differences in firm behavior during the period of the VRAs and the fuel economy regulations.

The long-run, direct price effects of the VRAs and fuel economy regulations can be approximated by summing the coefficients for the VRA and VRA1 variables in each of the price equations, above. These total effects are summarized in Table 12. Differences in overall firm strategy are immediately apparent in this table.

While the VRAs and the fuel economy regulations clearly resulted in substantial price increases at all three domestic firms, these price changes were not uniformly distributed across the domestic firms. The "big three" all raised their small car prices, though GM was not able to sustain as large an increase in its prices in this segment as were other firms. The VRAs and the fuel economy regulations induced changes in relative pricing and the distribution of products among size classes. Ford cut its intermediate prices, presumably in response to increased foreign competition in this segment, and increased its large car prices to maximize returns in this segment while reducing large car output (thus raising its fleet fuel economy averages).[29] GM's strategy was almost exactly the reverse of Ford's. GM responded to intermediate competition by raising prices and profits in this segment. This strategy seems to reveal a belief that the fuel economy regulations would eventually be relaxed and that there would be no need to change the composition of its output. The decline in GM's large car prices, in response to the VRAs, reflects the competitive problems of its large-car offerings, and possibly a decision to fill the gap left by Ford in the large car market, as well as a possible "bet" on the relaxation of the fuel economy regulations.

The contrast between Ford and GM in this case is striking. Faced with increased foreign competition in its intermediate product line and the threat of large taxes (fines) from the fuel economy regulations Ford introduces new intermediate products and downsizes its whole product mix. GM is slower to respond and builds its strategy around a belief that it can force the government to relax the CAFE standards, which it ultimately succeeds in doing.[30]

Further information about the market power of each of the domestic producers, by size class, is revealed in the estimated coefficients for changes in the average price of other cars (LGPBRxyy) in the domestic regressions described above. Table 13 reproduces the coefficient estimates for this variable in the output regressions and Table 14 shows the results for the Price regressions.

There is little effective product differentiation in the small car market, as reflected in the high correlation between own small car prices and LGPBRSyy discussed above and the in the negative coefficient on for LGPBRSyy for all four domestic firms in the output equations (Table 13). The output regressions suggest that Ford has substantial product differentiation in its medium car product lines, vis-a-vis other producers, as reflected in the positive coefficient for this variable. Results for Ford Large cars are insignificant, but GM does manage to achieve effective product differentiation in the large car market, as does Chrysler.[31]

TABLE 13

THE EFFECT OF THE AVERAGE PRICE OF OTHER CARS (LGPBRxyy) ON OUTPUT BY FIRM AND SIZE CLASS

Firm:	GM	FORD	CHRYSLER	AM
LGPBRxyy for:				
Small Cars	-1.072	-2.012	-0.325	-5.839
	(-1.376)	(-2.130)	(-0.396)	(-3.488)
Medium Cars	-0.246	2.204	-0.033	-4.692
	(-0.292)	(1.849)	(-0.025)	(-1.817)
Large Cars	1.697	0.204	2.239	
	(2.155)	(0.144)	(1.315)	

TABLE 14

THE EFFECT OF THE AVERAGE PRICE OF OTHER CARS (LGPBRxyy) ON OWN PRICE BY FIRM AND SIZE CLASS

Firm:	GM	FORD	CHRYSLER	AM
LGPBRxyy for:				
Small Cars	0.704	0.101	0.216	-0.457
	(3.763)	(0.653)	(1.505)	(-2.371)
Medium Cars	0.303	0.663	0.545	-0.086
	(2.892)	(2.346	(2.505)	(-0.268)
Large Cars	0.658	0.924	0.335	
	(3.531)	(1.697)	(1.307)	

The fact that the coefficients for LGPBRxyy in the price equations (Table 14) are all positive for each size class for each of the big three firms may reflect pricing coordination in the industry. This can reflect both strategic behavior and price-leadership relationships. The behavior is strategic if producers increase their own prices when the average prices of other cars rises. An alternative response would be to maintain or reduce prices, in order to increase sales.[32] Price leadership would lead to smaller coefficients for the LGPBRxyy term for the price leader than for follower firms. These results suggest that GM might have been the price leader in the medium and large car markets.

These interpretations on market structure should be viewed as working research questions. More specific tests, using direct estimates of the elasticities of residual demand curves, would be needed to test market structure or conduct hypotheses. These results suggest that further research in this area might be productive.

E. Summary

The results on the direct effects of the VRAs which have been presented in this chapter provided tests of several competing hypotheses about the effects of trade protection in this industry. The VRAs clearly led to price increases for most domestic producers, in most size classes, as shown in Table 12 above and in the individual results by size class. The price effects were statistically significant in most cases. The VRAs increased sales for some firms in some size classes and decreased sales in other classes. The VRAs were associated with short-run increases in the output of small cars, but reductions in the output of medium and large cars. The analysis of quantity effects is complicated by the indirect effects of the VRAs on prices, factor costs and output, and by other policies, most significant among those being the fuel economy regulations, which may also have changed the level and composition of domestic output. The direct and indirect effects of the VRAs, and their affects on employment in the domestic auto industry are examined in Chapter VI.

NOTES

1. If labor markets were perfectly competitive and firms were cost minimizers, then we would not expect the VRAs to have any effects on wage rates. A wage model is developed here which includes the VRAs as explanatory variables.

2. The total market share of the 4 U.S. auto producers average 82.8% in the 1970s and 73.4% in the 1980s. The 4-firm concentration ratios would be slightly higher, in both periods because the largest import supplier's sales usually exceeded those of American Motors.

3. Crandall, *et al*, 1986, p.126.

4. *ibid*, p.138.

5. *ibid*, p.138.

6. *ibid*, p.137-138.

7. Large cars were not soil in the U.S. by AM during the period of the quotas, so these equations are estimated only for small and medium AM cars.

8. The level of output can fall if protection increases a firm's market power. If demand is linear, an increase in market power would be reflected in an increase in the *slope* of a firm's residual demand curve.

9. A complete labor and capital cost series was not available for the American Motors Corporation, as noted in Chapter III. Therefore AM factor costs are not included in this model.

10. The critical value of the t-test at the 20% level with 50 degrees of freedom is 1.30 (Pindyck and Rubinfeld, 1981, p.608).

11. Only small and medium car equations were estimated for AM, as noted above.

12. The rationale for choosing these particular variables in presented in Chapters III and IV.

13. As noted above, the VRAs were formally enacted in April of 1981 and tariffs on Japanese truck imports were effectively increased in August, 1980. Review of the price data reported in Chapter 4 suggests that domestic auto manufacturers substantially increased prices in the 1981 model year (which begins in 1980:IV). This shift probably reflects both higher imported truck prices due to the increase in tariffs on small Japanese trucks, and the anticipated effects of auto import controls which were known to be under consideration in 1980.

14. See note 26 (Chapter II) for a review of the VRA limits.

15. There are three size classes and four domestic firms. However, AM did not produce large cars in the 1980s, so the models were only estimated for small and medium AM cars. Thus there are 11 domestic price equations, 11 domestic quantity equations, 1 import price and 1 import quantity equation in the model.

16. The terms "significant" and "insignificant" are used hereinafter to refer to a *t*-test on the results for particular regression coefficients. The significance level (20%, 10%, 5% or 1%) will generally be specified. "Weakly significant" will sometimes be used to refer to a coefficient which is significantly different from zero at only the 20% confidence level. "Strongly significant" will sometimes be used to refer to a coefficient which is significantly different from zero at the 1% confidence level.

17. *t*-statistics for each coefficient are report in parentheses below the parameter estimate in each table of regression results in this chapter.

18. An alternative interpretation of the sign of the coefficient for LGPBRSyy is that it reflects the reaction of the firm (and of all other firms) to a change in the average price of cars. This interpretation is based on the observation that the residual demand elasticity is the sum of the structural demand elasticity and the reaction-function responses from other firms to a change in a firm's own quantity or price. This interpretation would suggest that firms reduce output, in response to a change in LGPBRSyy, in order to increase their own price and profits. Both views support the conclusion that the domestic auto industry is a tight oligopoly, which has maintained effective control over prices in this period and has few problems with cheating.

19. Takacs and Tanzer (1981) found that changes in gas prices and the gas crises had positive effects on domestic subcompact sales. This result could be tested at the firm level by desegregating small car sales in this study into its subcompact and compact components.

20. After-tax profits rose at Ford during the 1985-1987 period, while profit peaks for GM and Chrysler came in 1984 and 1985, as shown in the following data.

After-Tax Income
(Millions of Current Dollars)

year	GM	Ford	Chrysler	total
1980	-762.5	-1543.3	-1709.7	-4015.5
1981	333.4	-1060.1	-475.6	-1202.3
1982	962.7	-657.8	-68.9	236.0
1983	3730.2	1866.9	301.9	5899.0
1984	4516.5	2906.8	1496.1	8919.4
1985	3999.0	2515.4	1635.2	8149.6
1986	2944.7	3285.1	1403.6	7633.4
1987	3550.9	4625.2	1289.7	9465.8

Source:　　　　　　Standard and Poor's Compustat Services, Inc., Income Before Extraordinary Items (Compustat data item 18).

21. The own-wage effects from Table 4, which are discussed here, are not significant for Ford and only weakly significant for Chrysler. These results may simply reflect an identification problem. The results in this research generally do not consistently lead to the rejection of the hypothesis that labor markets are competitively structured in the auto industry, despite unionization and the high level of wages relative to other U.S. manufacturing industries (Crandall, 1984).

22. The discussion here refers to the direct effect, as reflected in the coefficient for the VRA dummy variables. Actual price changes for each manufacturers reflect changes in the prices of all other cars, macro variables and factor costs, as well as the (direct and indirect) VRA effects.

23. It is important to point out that the price series used for this study are based on published wholesale prices for cars, and do not reflect the effects of manufacturer rebates, discounted financing and other sales promotions, which do reduce the effective prices paid for cars.

24. Henderson (1985), p. 45-46

25. This point is confirmed in a regression run by Crandall, *et al* (1986), which shows that "...it is clear that GM has made the greatest progress in improve fuel efficiency since 1970, given the weight of its cars (p.130)".

26. It has also been suggested that Chrysler was severely constrained in large car production capacity in the early 1980s, which may have also motivated their 1981 product re-alignment.

27. Factors other than the gas crises may have been responsible for the ways in which the two gas-crises affected import auto prices. The costs of auto pollution controls rose dramatically in the past-1973 period, putting upward pressure on all auto prices. The value of the dollar began to rise following the U.S. Federal Reserve Bank's tightening of monetary policy in October, 1979, which reduced the delivered cost of imports. However, changes in the structure of the import market between 1973 (when only three Japanese firms were competitive enough to sell more than 100,000 cars per year in the U.S.) and 1979 (when five Japanese firms exceeded 100,000 units in U.S. sales) remains an important explanatory variable.

28. Changes in the number of hours worked per employee year will also change average total compensation per employee, even if hourly labor costs are constant.

29. Note that the decline in Ford's intermediate prices was probably exaggerated in this sample because new product offerings such as Taurus/Sable did not appear in its line until 1986. It may have cut prices on older, less costly models during the early 1980s to build its customer base in anticipation of the new model introductions.

30. Note that GM was also downsizing its product line and increasing fleet fuel economy much more rapidly than the other domestic producers, throughout the 1970s and 1980s (Crandall, *et al*, 1986, pp.127-132).

31. However, shortages in large car production capacity at Chrysler apparently limited its ability to compete in this market segment during the study period, thus limiting the meaningful result to the GM case.

32.   On the other hand, if all producers are subject to external requirements (i.e., pollution and safety standards) which causes all prices to rise at the same time, then this positive relationship could be the result of a competitive market structure. It is important to note that both LGPBRxyy and LOGPxyy are real price series.

CHAPTER VI
SIMULATION AND POLICY ANALYSIS

In this Chapter the model estimated in Chapter V is used to estimate the total (direct + indirect) effect of the VRAs on prices, output and employment in the U.S. auto industry. This Chapter will show that the period of the VRAs was associated with substantial increases in the average prices of all cars. Overall, the VRAs were also associated with a *loss* in domestic output. However, this effect is more properly described as the result of the combined effects of the VRAs *and other policy restrictions which affected the domestic auto industry during this time period.* A major task in this Chapter is the separation of the effects of the VRAs from those of other policies, most importantly the Government's fuel economy regulations.

One of the surprising results in this research is that the largest output effect associated with the VRAs was a major reduction in large-car sales (in terms of both the percentage change in output due to the VRAs, and the absolute change in output). Economic theory, and empirical research by Feenstra (1984, 1985a and 1985b) and others suggests that the VRAs have their biggest effects in the small- and medium-sized car markets.

It is not at all clear that the VRAs *caused* the estimated reduction in the output of domestic large cars found in this Chapter. The VRAs clearly increased the market power of the domestic industry, essentially cartelizing Japanese producers and limiting competitive pressures facing domestic firms, allowing them to substantially raise prices on all products. However, consumer preferences for big cars may have been reduced by the two gas crises of the 1970s, and fuel economy regulations clearly created incentives for domestic auto producers to downsize, reduce large car output and increase domestic production of small cars (Henderson, 1985). These three factors (the VRAs, gas crises and fuel economy regulations) combined to change both relative prices and relative market shares of small, medium and large cars. Furthermore, their combined effects varied substantially across firms,

115

suggesting that strategy had important effects on outcomes. By disaggregating to three size classes, at the firm level, this Chapter will develop some inferences about the relative importance of each of these three factors. This Chapter will also show that disaggregated analysis is essential for accurate forecasting of auto industry output, because the nature of competition and the patterns of demand differ widely across car size classes.

The model simulation procedure is described in section A, below. Section B presents the results of the simulations for the U.S. auto market, including the effects of the VRAs on factor prices. This section analyzes the Price and Output effects which were associated with the VRAs (in percentage terms). Section C summarizes the output effects of the VRAs in terms of the overall number of cars produced in the U.S., under various assumptions about the effects of the other factors, and then estimates the employment impacts of the VRAs, under these assumptions. Chapter VII will then summarize the lessons of this research for public policy development in for the auto industry.

A. Model Simulation

Price and output equations for each of the domestic producers, for each of three size classes of cars, and for total imports were estimated in Chapter V (equations 6 and 7). The general form of those equations was:

(1) $\quad Q_i = a_1 + \alpha_1 P_j + \alpha_2 Y + \alpha_3 W + \alpha_4 W_I + \alpha_5 W_i + \varepsilon_1,$

(2) $\quad P_i = b_1 + \beta_1 P_j + \beta_2 Y + \beta_3 W + \beta_4 W_I + \beta_5 W_i + \varepsilon_2,$

12 price and 12 output equations were estimated in Chapter V.[1] When (1) and (2) are viewed as a system of equations which determines equilibrium in the domestic auto market, the cross price and factor cost terms (P_j, W_I and W_i) are all endogenous. The policy dummy variables VRA and VRA1 are components of the vector Y, as explained above.

Seven factor cost equations of the following general form were also estimated:

(3) $\qquad\qquad\qquad FC_i = c_1 + \Gamma_1 Y + \Gamma_2 W + \varepsilon_3,$

The seven factors included firm-specific capital and labor costs (per employee) for GM, Ford and Chrysler and a measure of the total hourly cost (including fringe benefits) of unionized labor in the U.S.

These 31 equations, together with a number of identities used to define the average price (P_j) variables and to calculate the anti-logarithms of the estimated logs of P and Q, form the model of the auto industry used in this Chapter. This system of equations was used to simulate output and prices in the domestic auto industry, with and without the VRAs. The model was too large and complicated to be solved in reduced form. The SIML routine, a part of the TSP econometric package, was used instead to simulate the effects of changes in policy variables (VRA and VRA1) on P, Q and factor cost variables.

The simulations were carried out in three stages, to isolate the effects of different variables on Price and Quantity in each case. *Stage 1* simulations estimated each of the 24 Price and Output variables, with and without the VRA effects, holding all other prices and factor costs constant. *Stage 2* simulations estimated P and Q, with and without the VRAs, while allowing the average prices of other cars (LGPBRxyy in Chapter V) to vary over the simulations. *Stage 3* simulations take into account changes in factor costs and related changes in firm strategic price and output behavior resulting from the VRAs. The Stage 1 results reflect the direct effects of the VRAs on Price and Output, while Stage 2 and 3 include the direct *and* indirect effects. Stage 2 simulates the effects that higher average prices would have on demand in each market segment, in the absence of factor cost changes and strategic behavior on the part of market participants. Stage 3 reflects the combined effects of changes in factor costs and product market interactions on equilibria with and without the VRAs. These simulations show that market outcomes are highly sensitive to factor cost changes and related shifts in strategic behavior.

B. Simulation Results

The results for price and quantity changes, with and without the VRAs, are presented here for two periods. The short-run effects are the predicted changes in P and Q resulting from the first three years of the VRAs (from 1980:IV to 1983:IV). These changes reflect the direct and indirect (Stages 1-3) effects of the VRA dummy variable. The model was simulated with and without the VRA dummy, and the average changes in Q and P resulting from the VRAs are presented in Tables 1 and 2, below.[2] The long-run effects are defined here to be the predicted effects of the VRAs on P and Q in the last 11 quarters of the study period (1984:1 to 1986:3).[3] The long-run effects thus reflect the direct and indirect effects of both the VRA and VRA1 dummy variables. The long-run results are presented in Tables 3 and 4, below.

These simulations estimate the effects of the VRAs on output and prices at the firm level, given the actual historical values of all the other variables in the model (such as real income, gasoline prices, and interest rates) which were observed in the 1981-86 period. The base case is thus a prediction of what output and price levels would have been if the VRAs had not been in effect, given the observed levels of the exogenous variables in the model.

1. Short-run Output Effects of the VRAs

a. Small Cars. In the short-run the VRAs substantially increased the output of small cars, relative to the predicted output levels without the VRAs, as shown in Table 1. The direct (Stage 1) effect of the VRAs was positive for all firms, as noted in Chapter V.

TABLE 1
QUANTITY SIMULATIONS: INITIAL EFFECTS
(Average Change from the VRAs over 1981:I to 1984:IV)

Size Class/ Firm	Stage 1 Effect	Stage 2 Effect	Stage 3 Effect
Small-GM	9.9	-26.9%	-0.8%
Small-Ford	50.8%	74.8%	43.7%
Small-Chrysler	46.4%	42.7%	68.8%
Small-AM	161.4%	179.3%	144.5%
Medium-GM	15.5%	-1.8%	4.8%
Medium-Ford	-32.2%	-42.1%	-47.7%
Medium-Chrysler	16.1%	-48.7%	-10.3%
Medium-AM	201.7%	892.3%	521.1%
Large-GM	-22.7%	-44.8%	-30.9%
Large-Ford	15.8%	-24.0%	11.9%
Large-Chrysler	-22.6%	-25.6%	-31.7%
Total-GM	-0.4%	-27.0%	-10.6%
Total-Ford	12.3%	2.9%	-2.3%
Total-Chrysler	28.3%	11.0%	31.3%
Total-AM	161.4%	246.2%	192.1%
Total-Domestic	7.6%	-16.4%	-4.5%
Total Import	-29.1%	-29.1%	6.3%

Among the indirect effects, the average price of all other cars (LGPBRSyy) was lower with the VRAs because there was a substantial decline in large car sales associated with the VRAs, which increased small car sales and reinforced the direct VRA effect for Ford and Chrysler. The largest indirect effect in stage 2 resulted from the direct effect of the VRAs on import prices (which were about 40% higher with the VRAs in the short-run in Stage 1). Higher import prices reduced output for GM (substantially) and Chrysler (to a lesser extent) and increased output for Ford and AM, resulting in the observed changes between stages 1 and 2 in small car output.

Overall, changes in factor costs and related firm strategies under the VRAs appear to have had large effects on the small car output of each of the "big three" firms, as shown in the stage 3 results. The effect of the VRAs increased almost 30 percentage points for GM when the link between the VRAs and factor costs was considered, offsetting the negative effects of higher import prices on its small car production.[4] The effect of the VRAs on Ford output is reduced, and the effect on Chrysler is increased, between stages 2 and 3.

In the final short-run simulations (Stage 3) the direct and indirect effects of the VRAs stimulated small car output for Ford, Chrysler and AM, in inverse proportion to market share. The final simulations show that the VRAs slightly reduced small car output at GM, and increased output by 44% at Ford, by 69% at Chrysler and by 144% at AM. Thus the VRAs had a bigger effect on the output of the smaller, or fringe, competitors in the small car market.

b. Intermediate Cars. The direct effect of the VRAs was to increase intermediate output at GM, Chrysler and AM. The model also suggests that the VRAs substantially decreased intermediate car output at Ford in the short-run. However, there were unusual increases in Ford-large car output in the short-run, which may have reflected the particular strategic choices made by Ford under the VRAs and the fuel economy regulations. This effect is so surprising large (given that it is a short-run effect) that it must be flagged as suspect in this analysis.[5]

The indirect effects of price and factor cost changes associated with the VRAs reinforced the decline in Ford's intermediate output. Indirect effects (stages 2 and 3) reduced the positive effect of the VRAs on GM's intermediate output and resulted in a net loss in intermediate output for Chrysler. Only AM's intermediate output sustained a substantial *rate* of growth under the VRAs, in the short-run, but its output levels were small relative to the other three producers.

In the short-run total intermediate car output was reduced by the VRAs. Most of this reduction occurred at Ford, which could reflect strategic decisions and timing problems. Ford's output decline may represent a strategic choice to reallocate resources into the large-sized car class, because of GM's declining large car sales (which were related to GM's difficulty in meeting the CAFE standards in the 1983-85 period[6]). The problems at Ford could have also been magnified by differences in model vintage across manufacturers. Ford's new intermediate products did not come out until the end of the estimation period (1986). The VRA-induced move of Japanese producers into intermediate car production should not have had a significant effect on domestic intermediate sales in the short-run, because of the amount of time required to design and produce new, larger models. Thus other factors (strategy, timing and possibly estimation errors) are probably more important than the trade restraints in explaining the estimated drop in Ford's intermediate output which was associated with the VRAs in this model.

   c. Large Cars. The VRAs were associated with a direct-effect (stage 1) reduction in large car output of one-third at GM and Chrysler in the short-run. It is unlikely that the VRAs alone could have been responsible for this effect on large car output in the short-run. There are at least two plausible alternative explanations for these results. First, the fuel economy regulations encouraged these firms to downsize their product mix. Second, the downsizing could have also been caused by a lagged effect of higher gasoline prices on large-car demand. An alternative view is that the VRAs (or the CAFE standards) so increased the market power of domestic producers that it was to their advantage to significantly restrict output and raise prices and profits in this market segment. In general, a shift in preferences would be more likely to reduce prices, while the VRA and CAFE effects would lead to price increases. Thus, the price effects of the VRAs will provide additional information about the causes of the large-car output reductions.

   The direct effect of the VRAs was to increase large car output at Ford in the short-run. Again, it is hard to see why the output of large cars would increase in the short-run in response to the VRAs. This result probably represents a strategic shift in model mix on Ford's part, reflecting either: 1) Ford, acting as a fringe competitor, filling the demand for large cars vacated by GM and Chrysler; or 2) a belief by Ford that the CAFE standards would be relaxed and that higher output levels would increase pressure on the government to eliminate the CAFE penalties.[7] It is also possible that consumer preferences for Ford cars, vis-a-vis other domestic makes, rose in this period because of higher perceived quality or newer models.

   The negative direct effect of the VRAs on large car output for GM and Chrysler was reinforced by indirect changes in the prices of other cars. Factor cost changes and strategy shifts under the VRAs partially offset these direct and price-related output losses for GM, and they reinforced the effects of price changes and the VRAs at Chrysler. Price increases tended to reduce the benefits of the VRAs for Ford, but the total (stage 3) effect was still reflected a substantial increase in Ford's large car output. In the final simulations, the VRAs increased large car output at Ford by about 11% in the short-run, and reduced output by more than 30% at GM and at Chrysler.

d. Total Output Effects, by Firm. In the short run, the VRAs were associated with increases in total output at Chrysler and AM, and decreases at Ford and GM. Total domestic output was reduced by about 4.5% by the VRAs. However, much of the decline at GM was in the large car segments. If changes in large car output are ignored, or are assumed to be the result of other factors (the fuel economy regulations), then the VRAs also increased the output of GM's small and intermediate cars. The total short-run output increase was about 375,623 small and intermediate units at GM, C and AM. There was an output decline of 115,010 small and intermediate-sized units at Ford. However, the Ford decline is entirely due to the surprising decline in its intermediate-car output which was associated with the VRAs. The effects of the VRAs on the total number of cars produced in the U.S. are discussed in more detail in Section C, below.

e. Imports. The direct effect of the VRAs was to substantially reduce import sales in the U.S., in the short-run, as shown in Table 1. However changes in U.S. factor costs and the strategies of all producers, associated with the VRAs, completely offset the direct effects on imports, so that the final model predicts that imports would have been *slightly lower* if the VRAs had not been in effect. This effect may be related to increases in domestic prices which resulted from the VRAs.[8]

2. Short-run Price Effects of the VRAs

The prices of small cars made by the "Big Three" U.S. auto producers were all increased by the VRAs in the short-run, as shown in Table 2. The biggest increase was for Ford Small Cars, followed by Chrysler and then GM. The size and ranking of these direct effects were unchanged in the final simulations (Stage 3). American Motor's small car prices were essentially unchanged by the VRAs.

GM took the lead in initiating price increases for its intermediate-sized cars in the initial period of the VRAs, and was the only domestic producer to raise prices in this size-class in the short-run. Ford's intermediate prices fell dramatically, reflecting competitive problems with its intermediate product lines, as did American Motor's. Chrysler's intermediate prices were reduced slightly by the VRAs. Again, there was little difference between the initial and final simulations on the price side of the intermediate market.

TABLE 2
PRICE SIMULATIONS: INITIAL EFFECTS
(Average Change from the VRAs over 1981:I to 1984:IV)

Size Class/ Firm	Stage 1 Effect	Stage 2 Effect	Stage 3 Effect
Small-GM	9.9%	8.6%	10.6%
Small-Ford	20.5%	26.9%	21.4%
Small-Chrysler	11.7%	15.0%	13.8%
Small-AM	5.2%	4.3%	1.8%
Medium-GM	11.1%	13.2%	14.0%
Medium-Ford	-17.7%	-18.2%	-19.3%
Medium-Chrysler	0.7%	-7.6%	-1.8%
Medium-AM	-16.7%	-21.1%	-14.3%
Large-GM	3.2%	1.8%	4.1%
Large-Ford	3.6%	19.8%	5.9%
Large-Chrysler	5.6%	0.7%	0.6%
Total-GM	3.2%	2.6%	4.3%
Total-Ford	-3.5%	-5.3%	-5.5%
Total-Chrysler	5.6%	1.7%	1.7%
Total-AM	-8.3%	5.4%	2.5%
Total-Domestic	1.0%	-0.3%	0.7%
Total-Import	42.3%	42.3%	7.4%

The VRAs were also associated with price increases for all domestic large cars. The increases were not as big as those for small cars, and may have been more related to fuel economy regulations than to export restraints, for reasons noted above.

Average revenue *across all product lines* was increased only slightly in the short-run by the VRAs for GM, Chrysler and AM because of changes in product mix. The VRAs and the fuel economy regulations were associated with increased small car output and reduced large car output, as shown above, resulting in downward pressure on the size and value of the average unit sold. However, prices in every size class at GM were increased by the VRAs, and its average revenue per unit rose slightly. Small cars made up a very large proportion of Chrysler's output in the early 1980s (close to 80% of its units sales in 1981), so the changes in mix had a smaller effect on its average price. Average Prices at Ford were actually reduced by the VRAs, in the short-run, largely because of the large decline in both the output and the prices of its intermediate models.

Changes in the national model mix, associated with the VRAs and the fuel economy regulations limited their impact on *average* prices across all models in the short-run. However, the prices of all small and large cars, and of GM intermediates all rose significantly.

The direct effect of the VRAs was to substantially increase the prices of *imported* cars. However, after the indirect effects are accounted for, the stage 3 import price increase was only 7%. Note that this is an estimate of the short-run effect of the VRAs on *wholesale* prices. Retail import price increases were reported to be much larger than this in some parts of the country.

3. Long-run Quantity Effects of the VRAs

a. Small Cars. Table 3 shows that the (direct, stage 1) positive effects of the VRAs on small car output decline in the long-run (relative to Table 1) for Ford, Chrysler and AM, and increase in the long-run for GM. Only GM and Chrysler small-car output was increased directly in the long-run (in stage 1) by the VRAs. However, when price, strategy and factor cost changes are taken into account (stage 3), the VRAs and fuel economy regulations led to increased small car output at all four domestic firms in the long-run. In the final (stage 3) simulations GM's small car sales were about 13% higher with the VRAs in the long-run (versus -1% in the short-run). Ford's output increased by about one-third (versus 44% in the short-run). Chrysler's sales were increased by 45% because of protection (69% in the short-run) and AM's by 22% (145% in the short-run). Thus, despite some signs of decay, the positive effects of the VRAs and fuel economy regulations on domestic output did persist in the small car market for at least 5 years, despite higher prices for both import and domestic small cars.

b. Intermediate cars. The VRAs and other policy measures in effect in the mid-1980s increased the sales of intermediates for GM, Chrysler and AM in the long-run. The long-run results for Ford are still an anomaly, with large VRA-associated reductions in its intermediate output. The VRAs were expected to reduce sales of intermediate-sized cars, because they encouraged Japanese producers to move up into larger and higher-priced models. However, the fuel economy regulations and higher gas prices in the late 1970s encouraged firms to reduce the average sizes of their cars. Some firms converted products which had been large cars in the 1970s into intermediates (such as the Ford LTD '83) in the 1980s. The model simulated here predicts the net impact of these two policies, one tending to increase mid-sized car demand (the fuel economy regulations) and the other tending to reduce it (the VRAs). The CAFE effect dominated output at GM, Chrysler and AM. The VRA effect appears to have been the most important determinant of Ford's intermediate output in the long-run, although the statistical significance of this effect is low (20%).

TABLE 3
QUANTITY SIMULATIONS: LONG-RUN EFFECTS
(Average Change from the VRAs over 1984:1 to 1986:3)

Size Class/ Firm	Stage 1 Effect	Stage 3 Effect	Stage 4 Effect
Small-GM	13.7%	-9.3%	13.3%
Small-Ford	-4.7%	5.8%	33.4%
Small-Chrysler	24.8%	19.6%	44.5%
Small-AM	-32.1%	-28.8%	22.3%
Medium-GM	7.5%	-1.8%	0.7%
Medium-Ford	-27.4%	-29.5%	-43.6%
Medium-Chrysler	-8.0%	-39.7%	28.3%
Medium-AM	810.8%	228.5%	1576.4%
Large-GM	-57.1%	-58.7%	-42.7%
Large-Ford	-34.7%	-41.0%	18.6%
Large-Chrysler	-71.0%	-65.2%	-64.7%
Total-GM	-23.8%	-31.2%	-14.3%
Total-Ford	-20.1%	-20.0%	-5.8%
Total-Chrysler	5.1%	-11.2%	30.8%
Total-AM	-32.1%	-15.9%	41.1%
Total-Domestic	-20.1%	-26.1%	-6.7%
Total-Import	-39.0%	-38.3%	-10.4%

In the final (stage 3) simulations, the period of the VRAs was associated with an output increase of about 1% for GM intermediates (versus a 5% increase in the short run). Ford suffered a loss of about 44% of output (48% in the short run). Chrysler intermediates gained about 28% in the long-run under the VRAs (versus a decline of about 10% in the short-run) and AM increased sales 15-fold in the long-run (5-fold in the short-run), from a very small base. American Motor's intermediate sales were also dominated by captive imports from Renault, which may also reflect the effects of the VRAs.

Overall sales of domestic intermediates were reduced by the VRAs and fuel economy regulations by about 235,000 units in the long-run. The decline in Ford's output in this market segment more than offset gains at other firms.

c. Large Cars. The short-run patterns of sharp decline in large car output for GM and Chrysler persist in the long-run in this model. The direct effects are very large for these two firms. In the final simulations GM large car sales are reduced by about 43% and Chrysler's by nearly two-thirds. These effects are even larger than the corresponding short-run impacts (-31% and -32%, respectively). Again, however, the fuel-economy-related incentives for firms to downsize probably played a more important role than did the VRAs in these results.

Ford's large car output increased by about 19%, relative to trend, in the long run (versus 12% in the short-run).

d. Total Output Effects, by Firm. In the long-run the VRAs were associated with reductions in total output at GM and Ford, and increases at Chrysler and AM. Overall U.S. output was reduced by the VRAs by about 7%. However, the entire output decline at GM was in its large-car lines, and the entire decline at Ford was in its mid-sized car sales. It is not clear that these two results were caused by the VRAs. The quantity effects of the VRAs are analyzed more closely in Section C, below.

e. Imports. The VRAs were clearly a binding constraint on import sales in the 1984-1986 period. This model estimates that import sales were about 10% lower than they would otherwise have been without the VRAs. Lost import sales totaled about 470,000 units in the 1986 model year. However, *transplant production* by Japanese-based assemblers was not included in this model. In 1986 233,000 units were assembled in the U.S. by Japanese-based assemblers. None of these producers were assembling any cars in the U.S. prior to 1983, so it is reasonable to assume that the VRAs (and the more general threat of trade protection in the late 1970s) were responsible for the decisions made to assemble Japanese cars in the U.S. Transplant production is an important factor in the total employment impact of the Trade Restraints. Transplant assembly will grow rapidly in the 1990s in North America, according to plans already announced for new assembly plants, which will dramatically change the nature of competition and the demands for protection in the domestic auto market in the future.

4. Long-run Price Effects of the VRAs

The prices of small cars made by the Big Three U.S. auto producers were all increased by the VRAs in the long-run as shown in Table 4. The biggest increase was for Ford small cars, followed by Chrysler and then GM. This was true of both the direct effects and the final simulations (Stage 3). The final price increases were slightly smaller in the long-run than in the short-run (i.e. 9% long-run vs. 11% short-run for GM). American Motors small car prices fell slightly in the long-run under the VRAs.

GM maintained its increased mid-sized car prices in the long-run, though at a slightly lower level (11% vs. 14%) than in the short-run, and Chrysler's intermediate prices were also increased by the VRAs in the long-run. The decline in Ford's intermediate prices found in the short-run was cut by about one third, to about -12%. Either Ford faced continuing competitive difficulties in this segment, or it decided to reclassify (and enlarge) some of its intermediates as large cars (thus lowering the average price of the remaining models).[9] The gain in Ford large car sales was much smaller than its losses in the mid-sized market, so factors other than product realignment reduced overall demand for Ford intermediates. American Motors had a much smaller price decrease in the long-run than it did in the short-run results (-3% vs. -14%).

TABLE 4
PRICE SIMULATIONS: LONG-RUN EFFECTS
(Average Change from the VRAs over 1984:1 to 1986:3)

Size Class/ Firm	Stage 1 Effect	Stage 3 Effect	Stage 4 Effect
Small-GM	5.4%	3.9%	8.7%
Small-Ford	26.9%	20.6%	18.7%
Small-Chrysler	22.2%	19.3%	13.7%
Small-AM	-1.3%	-1.5%	-1.6%
Medium-GM	15.0%	14.0%	11.3%
Medium-Ford	-17.2%	-14.3%	-12.2%
Medium-Chrysler	6.6%	1.4%	5.6%
Medium-AM	-6.9%	-8.3%	-3.1%
Large-GM	-2.1%	-2.4%	-.6%
Large-Ford	27.0%	25.8%	13.4%
Large-Chrysler	-1.9%	-1.9%	-1.5%
Total-GM	-7.9%	-7.0%	-2.3%
Total-Ford	4.4%	1.4%	-1.6%
Total-Chrysler	9.4%	1.9%	7.5%
Total-AM	-4.7%	5.3%	4.5%
Total-Domestic	-3.8%	-4.5%	-2.0%
Total-Import	28.0%	20.0%	6.1%

GM maintained its increased mid-sized car prices in the long-run, though at a slightly lower level (11% vs. 14%) than in the short-run, and Chrysler's intermediate prices were also increased by the VRAs in the long-run. The decline in Ford's intermediate prices found in the short-run was cut by about one third, to about -12%. Either Ford faced continuing competitive difficulties in this segment, or it decided to reclassify (and enlarge) some of its intermediates as large cars (thus lowering the average price of the remaining models).[10] The gain in Ford large car sales was much smaller than its losses in the mid-sized market, so factors other than product realignment reduced overall demand for Ford intermediates. American Motors had a much smaller price decrease in the long-run than it did in the short-run results (-3% vs. -14%).

The VRAs were also associated with increases in the price of GM, and Ford large cars in the long-run. The increases at each firm were smaller than those for small cars, and were probably caused fuel economy regulations and not the export restraints, for reasons noted above. The increase was smaller than in the short-run for GM, but larger than in the short-run for Ford. Ford achieved both higher prices and higher large-car output levels during the VRAs, while GM had a much smaller price increase and a decline in large-car sales. These results largely explain the growth in total profits at Ford, relative to GM, in the mid 1980s (see note 20, Chapter V, above).

Average revenue across all product lines was reduced slightly by the VRAs for GM and Ford because of changes in product mix. Nonetheless, it remains true that prices in every size class at GM rose were increased by the VRAs, even though the *average revenue* per unit was smaller with the VRAs in the long-run. Average revenue per unit at Ford was *reduced* by the VRAs, in the long-run, because of the big decline in both output and prices of intermediate models discussed above. Small cars made up a very large proportion of Chrysler's output in the early 1980s (close to 80% of its units sales in 1981), so its average revenue per unit was increased by about 7% by the VRAs in the long-run.

Changes in the national model mix, associated with the VRAs and fuel economy regulations, limited the impact of these policies on *average* prices in the long-run. However, the prices of most small and large cars, and of GM and Chrysler intermediates were all increased significantly by these policies.

The direct effect of the VRAs was to substantially increase the prices of *imported* cars. However, after the indirect effects are accounted for, the price increase in the final simulation was only about 6% (versus 7% in the short-run). Note, again, that this is an estimate of the effect of the VRAs on *wholesale* prices.

5. Factor Costs.

The VRAs and fuel economy regulations had significant effects on the costs of labor and capital, and these effects were different for each firm. The VRAs increased the total cost of hourly UAW Labor slightly in the short-run, and reduced it slightly in the long-run, as shown in Table 5. Total labor costs at GM increased under the VRAs. This could reflect higher white collar labor costs or increases in the ratio of management to production labor. Labor costs fell at Ford, by about 1 per cent. They fell by 4% at Chrysler in the short-run, as a result of the wage concessions made by Chrysler workers as part of the Chrysler bailout, and a reduction in the number of Chrysler managers. Chrysler's labor costs were only 2% lower in the long-run, as the bailout agreements expired and its labor contracts were renegotiated.

TABLE 5
THE EFFECTS OF THE VRAS ON LABOR COSTS
(Average Percent Change)

	Short-Run	Long-Run
GM	0.64%	3.97%
Ford	-0.85%	-1.19%
Chrysler	-3.71%	1.86%
United Auto Workers	0.18%	-0.12%

The coefficients for the effects of the VRAs on capital costs were much more (statistically) significant than those for labor costs. Changes in the real cost of capital can't be measured in percentage terms, because the base-case level of capital costs was very small and/or negative in some periods. Table 6 reports absolute changes in capital cost rates, averaged over the short- and long-run periods. The VRAs no significant effect on capital costs at GM in the short-run, but reduced capital cost (and profitability) in the long-run. The rise in GM's labor costs in the long-run and the problems in its large-car lines explain its decline in profitability in this period.

TABLE 6
THE EFFECTS OF THE VRAS ON CAPITAL COSTS
(Average Change in Capital Cost Rate)

	Short-Run	Long-Run
GM	0.04%	-1.22%
Ford	1.04%	1.67%
Chrysler	1.00%	0.58%

Ford, on the other hand, had a decline in its labor costs, and a rise in (highly profitable) large car output under the VRAs. Thus Ford's capital costs and profits were increased by the VRAs by about 1 percentage point in the short-run and 1.7 percentage points in the long-run. These are very significant changes, especially in view of the fact that the cost of borrowed funds probably decreased under the VRAs (as company risk fell), and therefore real returns to equity capital at Ford apparently increased by substantially more than the amounts reported in Table 6. These results casts further doubt on the model's prediction of a substantial decline in Ford's intermediate output, under the VRAs. Chrysler's capital costs (and profitability) were also increased under the

VRAs, though not by as much as at Ford, and the effect declines in the long-run at Chrysler.

In sum, the VRAs and fuel economy regulations were very good for Ford, both in terms of its labor costs and especially its profitability. Chrysler also benefitted, although those gains decline in the long-run and may have had as much to do with the Chrysler bailout and related labor concessions as with the VRAs. General Motors experienced higher labor costs, a reduction in large car output and a decline in its profit levels under the VRAs and the other policy measures in place in the mid-1980s.

C. Total Output and Employment Impacts of the VRAs

A number of factors affected the output levels of the domestic auto industry in the 1981-1986 period, including the VRAs. The other forces included fuel economy regulations, lagged responses to higher gasoline prices and a possible decline in the overall competitiveness of GM.[11] The fact that many unusual forces influenced output patterns and levels in the domestic industry makes it impossible to precisely estimate the effects of the VRAs on total domestic output and employment. However the model developed in this Chapter, combined with economic intuition about the expected effects of some of the other factors, can be used to provide a range of estimates of the impacts of the VRAs which are more detailed and have a stronger empirical bases than previous estimates.[12]

The final (Stage 3) simulations for the effects of the VRAs and other factors on total output in 1983 and 1986 (measured in units sold in the domestic market), by firm and size class, are summarized in Table 7. These years were chosen to be representative of the short- and long-run effects of the VRAs.

The most important problems in identifying the effects of the VRAs in these simulations occur in the market for large cars. This Chapter has presented data and analysis which suggests that factors other than the VRAs were responsible for most of the observed changes in large car output. The changes in large car output at GM and Chrysler occurred in the early stages of the VRA. It is unlikely that Japanese producers were able in the short-run to increase production of their intermediate luxury models, which were substitutes for domestic large cars, in sufficient quantity to have a substantial impact on the large car market. Higher gasoline prices, the CAFE standards and fuel economy regulations, and the decline of GM all contributed to the predicted decline in large car output resulting from the VRAs. There is also uncertainty about the effects of the VRAs on the intermediate market, because mid-sized cars are closer in characteristics to some of the larger imported models and because mid-size models are more fuel-efficient than large domestic cars.

TABLE 7
EFFECTS OF THE VRAS AND
FUEL ECONOMY REGULATIONS ON OUTPUT
(Difference between the estimated number of
units sold with and without the VRAs)

	1983:I to 1983:IV	1985:IV to 1986:III
Small Cars:		
GM	-10633	178906
Ford	253477	197475
Chrysler	249757	189554
AM	67110	9516
Intermediates:		
GM	62840	35720
Ford	-360407	-339325
Chrysler	-10853	58652
AM	17492	9964
Large Cars:		
GM	-549896	-798541
Ford	27953	43422
Chrysler	-38435	-27328
Transplants	31473	232954
Addenda: Total Domestic Sales	6301886	8123878

The most important problems in identifying the effects of the VRAs in these simulations occur in the market for large cars. This Chapter has presented data and analysis which suggests that factors other than the VRAs were responsible for most of the observed changes in large car output. The changes in large car output at GM and Chrysler occurred in the early stages of the VRA. It is unlikely that Japanese producers were able in the short-run to increase production of their intermediate luxury models, which were substitutes for domestic large cars, in sufficient quantity to have a substantial impact on the large car market. Higher gasoline prices, the CAFE standards and fuel economy regulations, and the decline of GM all contributed to the predicted decline in large car output resulting from the VRAs. There is also uncertainty about the effects of the VRAs on the intermediate market, because mid-sized cars are closer in characteristics to some of the larger imported models and because mid-size models are more fuel-efficient than large domestic cars.

1. Output Scenarios

A series of scenarios are developed here to provide a range of estimates for the overall effects of the VRAs alone on domestic output. One possible simplifying assumption is that only domestic small car production, 56% to 63% of total U.S. sales during the VRAs, was affected by the restraints.[13] This assumption (*Scenario A* in Table 8) implicitly presupposes that the VRAs themselves had no effect on the intermediate or large car markets. Under these assumptions, the VRAs increased domestic small car sales by 560,000 units in 1983, 8.9% of actual sales of all domestically built models in that year.[14] In 1986 the VRAs had a large effect on the number of units sold than in 1983 but the percentage change falls to 7.1% because total demand was much larger in 1986.

Scenario A leaves out the effects of transplant production in the U.S. *Scenario B* assumes that all Japanese production in the U.S. was the result of trade protection and it predicts that 1983 output would have been 9.4% lower if the VRAs had not been in place. By 1986 this figure increases to 10% because of the rapid growth of transplant production in the U.S. There was no production in Japanese owned auto facilities in the U.S. prior to 1983, but there were 4 plants operating by 1986, with several more planned for operation in the future. Increased transplant production in North America in the 1990s is likely to lead to renewed requests for protection in the domestic market, as discussed in the next Chapter.

A more conservative set of assumptions includes the intermediate market in the Scenarios. *Scenario C* simply incorporates the effects of the VRA policy variables on all domestic producers of intermediate cars. This substantially reduces the estimated effects of the VRAs to 4.6% of output in 1983 (292,000 units) and 7.1% of output in 1986. One problem with including all intermediates in Scenario C is that the estimate for the direct effects of the VRAs on Ford intermediates is only weakly significant (T-stat of -1.6), and is very large in magnitude. An alternative is to exclude the effects of the VRAs on mid-sized Fords and to include all other small and intermediate cars and transplants. *Scenario D* uses these assumptions. The net effects of the VRAs were positive for all other domestic intermediate producers, so this set of assumptions lead to an even higher estimate of the impact of the VRAs on domestic output than scenario A, 10.5% in 1983 and 11.2% in 1986.

Scenario D implies that on balance the VRAs helped producers of domestic intermediates in both the short- and the long-run.

TABLE 8
VRA IMPACT SCENARIOS
(Net effect (in units) of the VRAs on output
and share of actual domestic output)

Scenarios:		1983:I to 1983:IV	1985:IV to 1986:III
A.	Small Cars:		
	Total Change	559711	575451
	Output Share	8.9%	7.1%
B.	Small+Transplants:		
	Total Change	591184	808405
	Output Share	9.4%	10.0%
C.	Small+Int+Transplants:		
	Total Change	292176	573416
	Output Share	4.6%	7.1%
D.	Small+Int+Transplants: (except Ford Interm)		
	Total Change	660663	912741
	Output Share	10.5%	11.2%
E. All Domestic+Transplants:			
	Total Change	-268202	-209031
	Output Share	-4.3%	-2.6%

Scenarios A through D suggest that total domestic auto production would have declined by 4.6% to 10.5% if the VRAs had not been in place in 1983, and 7.1% to 11.2% in 1986. Thus the total effects of the restraints apparently grew over time, principally because of the rapid growth of transplant production in the mid-1980s. These effects on production by domestic producers, measured in terms of the output share, decline in all four scenarios between 1983 and 1986.

If the CAFE standards, higher gasoline prices and the secular decline in GM's market share are believed to be less important than the VRAs in explaining changes in large car output patterns in this period, then large cars should be included in estimates of the effects of the VRAs on the domestic industry. *Scenario E* estimates the total impact of the VRA-dummy variables and transplant production on auto output in the U.S. These results suggest that the VRAs *reduced* domestic output by 4.3% in 1983 and by 2.6% in 1986.

2. *Employment Impacts*

In order to calculate the employment effects of the VRAs it is necessary to distinguish sales of models produced in the U.S. from domestic *production* of those same models. There is a substantial trade flow in vehicles and parts between the U.S. and Canada. The U.S. was a net importer of cars from Canada in the 1980s, as shown in Table 9. Between 1% and 7% of "domestic" models sold here are net imports from Canada. Thus part of the employment benefits from the VRAs flow to Canadian workers, which must be taken into account when calculating the effects of the restraints on domestic employment.

The auto assembly sector, as defined by the Dept. of Commerce (S.I.C. 371), includes both auto and truck production. Total direct employment in and the output of this industry are shown in Table 9. Employment is shown from 1978 through 1986, to illustrate the loss in employment experienced since the last cyclical peak in 1978. 135,000 fewer workers were directly engaged in U.S. auto production in 1986 than in 1978. This decrease is almost entirely explained by the decline in factory sales of U.S. cars since labor productivity, measured in terms of output per worker (the inverse of column E), and truck sales were essentially identical in these two periods.[15]

Employment impacts were calculated assuming that the Canadian share of U.S. market would be unchanged in any given year, and that losses in output would lead to direct employment reductions at the average level of labor productivity which actually prevailed in any given year. Thus the output losses without the VRAs in each Scenario in Table 8 were multiplied by the parameters in Columns E and F to determine the number of job opportunities which would have been lost if the VRAs had not been in effect. These are the direct employment impacts reported in Table 10.

Crandall (1984 and 1986) and Feenstra (1984, 1985a and 1985b) assume that the average car which would be displaced by imports would be a subcompact, and that it would require 20% less labor for assembly than the average domestic model. This assumption would reduce all the figures in Table 10 by the same proportion (20%).[16]

For each persons directly employed in auto production the U.S. Department of Labor (1985) has estimated that there are approximately 2 additional workers are employed in upstream industries supplying parts and materials for auto production and in downstream service and distribution trades. This indirect employment has been ignored in most other studies of the employment impact of trade, but is clearly an important source of potential labor displacement which would result from increased auto imports.[17] Thus, on the basis of the assumptions

TABLE 9
EMPLOYMENT AND OUTPUT IN
THE U.S. MOTOR VEHICLE INDUSTRY

Year	Total Employment SIC 371 (000)	Factory Sales of US Cars	Factory Sales of US Trucks	Net Imports of Canadian Production Cars	Empl/Unit of US Production [A/(B+C)]	US Production Share of US Car Sales [B/(B+D)]
78	1000	9165190	3670897	300125	0.078	0.968
79	994	8419226	3004208	82588	0.087	0.990
80	794	6399840	1632898	87357	0.099	0.987
81	794	6255340	1700452	94663	0.100	0.985
82	702	5049184	1879180	369714	0.101	0.932
83	749	6739223	2387685	313347	0.082	0.956
84	847	7621176	3042888	486228	0.079	0.940
85	872	8002259	3356905	242506	0.077	0.971
86	865	7516189	3392885	279272	0.079	0.964
Column:	A	B	C	D	E	F

used in this study (scenarios A through D), it seems reasonable to conclude that 22,000 to 52,000 direct job opportunities would have been lost in auto assembly in 1983 if the VRAs had not been enacted and that an additional 44,000 to 104,000 jobs in other sectors of the economy would also have been jeopardized if nothing had been done in 1981 to curtail auto imports. These figures rise in the long-run to an average of direct 55,000 job opportunities, and an additional 110,000 indirect openings if the VRAs had not been implemented.

TABLE 10
EMPLOYMENT IMPACTS--DIRECT JOB OPPORTUNITIES
CREATED BY THE VRAS

Scenarios:	1983:I to 1983:iv	1985:IV to 1986:III
A. Small Cars:	43892	43994
B. Small+Transp	46360	61804
C. Small+Int+Tr	22912	43838
D. Small+Int+Transp (except Ford Intermeds.)	51808	69780
Average of A through D:	41243	54854
E. All Dom+Tran	-21032	-15981
Addenda: Employment impacts of Transplants:	2468	17810

These estimates can be contrasted with several other published figures in Table 11. The direct effects estimated in Table 10 are substantially larger than those estimated by Tarr and Morkre, Crandall and Feenstra, on average, and closer to the estimates of the USITC and the Commerce Department.

The direct labor impacts estimated in Table 10 are smaller than those reported in Scott (1988). Those earlier estimates were constructed as an *upper limit* on the potential for Japanese market penetration from some hypothetical examples of potential market shares. The estimates in Table 10 can be interpreted as the *mean* expected affect, assuming that the estimated parameters of the model are consistent approximations of the true parameters. Another important difference between the scenarios in Table 10 and the earlier estimates is that the hypothetical examples did not take into account the effects of the price increases for domestic autos which resulted from the VRAs, which were quite large within individual size classes, as seen above. Higher average prices resulting from the VRAs (holding all other policies constant) probably reduced overall domestic demand, but this effect was not identified in the simulations because other policies and demand determinants were also changing in the same period and as a result there was substantial downsizing of the domestic model mix. This suggests another possible scenario, involving artificially restrained prices and the VRAs. This scenario, which is future research, would predict what output patterns might have been if the VRAs had been combined with some type of formal or informal price and wage restraint agreement.

TABLE 11
DIRECT EMPLOYMENT CONTENT OF IMPORTS
DISPLACED BY THE VRAS

Source	Time Frame	Loss in Domestic Output (thousands)	Labor Content of Imports Displaced
Tarr and Morkre (1984)	1980-81	121	4,598
Feenstra (1984a)	1980-81	53 to 212	5,600 to 22,300
Crandall (1984)	1981-83	712	26,200
USITC (1985c)	1981-84	618	44,100
Commerce Dept. (1985)	1981-85	720 to 1,128	32,000 to 62,000
Scott (1988) [a]	1980-84	1,725 to 2,300	100,200 to 137,900

[a] employment estimate includes the effects of transplant production in U.S.

NOTES

1. Small, medium and large car equations were estimated for GM, Ford, Chrysler and AM (small and medium only), and one equation was estimated for total import P and one for import Q.

2. Estimated values of P and Q were calculated in two ways. *The VRA case* is the results of simulations run assuming that the dummy variable VRA = 1 in the test period (1980:IV-1983:IV). *The base case* assumes that VRA = 0 in the test period. The difference in the dependent variable in each case (VRA case-base case) was assumed to be the result of the VRA restrictions. The percentage change in the dependent variable was calculated relative to the base case (no restriction), and the results are shown in Tables 1-5, this chapter.

3. Both the VRA and VRA1 variables were set equal to zero for the long-run base case simulations.

4. Note that in Stage 3 the initial increase in import prices is much lower, again reflecting the final effects of factor costs and related firm strategies on prices and output.

5. The sizable quantity effect for intermediate Ford cars may be the result of specification errors and multicollinearity problems in the model. The share of intermediate cars in total Ford output peaked at about 50% in 1977, fell to a low of 14% in 1981:II, and then recovered to levels in the 25-30% range during the VRAs. Thus the negative coefficient for the VRA effect for Ford intermediates, which was only weakly significant (T-stat value of 1.60), could also reflect a lagged response to higher gasoline prices which were correlated with the decline in Ford's intermediate car output. It is likely that a small change in the initial date of the VRA effect (i.e., from 1980:IV to 1981:II) would yield a change in the sign of the VRA coefficient. The output share of Ford's large cars followed a similar pattern, yet the coefficient for the VRA effect in that case was positive. Thus the model's estimates of the effects of the VRAs on Ford's intermediate output are probably too high.

6. Crandall, *et al*, 1986.

7. Note that Ford's model mix in the 1980s was more heavily weighted with small and intermediate cars than was GM's, who thus had more to lose with the imposition of the CAFE penalties. In 1986 the share of large cars in Ford's output averaged about 20% while GM's large car share averaged about 28% of its output. Thus both firms may have been moving towards similar market positions (in terms of model mix), in response to the CAFE standards, with FM reducing its large car sales and Ford increasing theirs.

8. Note that the price variable used in the import equations did not change substantially in the absence of the VRAs, because of changes in the model mix in this period. Thus price effects at the size class level (which were obscured in the aggregate price variable used) were probably reflected in other coefficients in the model.

9. Note that the VRAs were associated with increases in the prices of Ford's large cars, suggesting that model reclassification (from intermediate to large car class) was not a significant determinant of changes in Ford prices in either market segment.

10. Note that the VRAs were associated with increases in the prices of Ford's large cars, suggesting that model reclassification (from intermediate to large car class) was not a significant determinant of changes in Ford prices in either market segment.

11. The decline of GM is, in part, the expected process of gradual decline of the dominant firm in a weak cartel which as been observed in other sectors in the past, such as the U.S. steel industry (U.S. Steel) and the international oil market (Saudi Arabia). A recent text in industrial organization summarized the economic perspective:

> "Many economists believe that cartels will not endure unless they tightly control some indispensable input or get government support. For, if a cartel earns profits, entry will occur...What it comes down to is that, from birth, cartels spread existing economic niches wider and may open up new ones. It often pays someone to put resources into them. In the process, cartels tend to lose their ground". (McGhee, 1988, p.127)

The large amounts of capital required to design, build and market a viable auto line constitutes one "indispensable input" to successful maintenance of an auto cartel, but entry and exit has also been strongly influenced by government policies, over the past century of auto industry development. Altshuler, *et at* argue that "[b]ecause of strong restraints on entry and exit, there are likely to be about as many auto makers 20 years from now as today (p.183)." However, competition among the exiting set of auto makers is likely to result in substantial realignments of market shares.

GM's problems may also be related to creeping inefficiencies which have developed in its internal structure which have limited GM's ability to innovate and keep up with the productivity growth standards of the industry. Evidence of inefficiencies is found in the unusual pattern of increased GM labor cost under the VRAs, and reduced capital costs and profitability, in contrast to trends in the smaller domestic firms, especially Ford. These inefficiencies are another long-run cost of the cartel-like structure of the domestic auto market.

12. Previous studies of the economic effects of the VRAs include Crandall (1984 and 1986), Gomez-Ibanez et al (1983) and Mannering and Winston (1987).

13. The small car class in this study includes by compacts and subcompacts.

14. These scenarios are presented relative to predicted output with the VRAs to facilitate calculation of employment impacts.

15. Note that real value added per worker increased between 1978 and 1985 because of the increase in the average value per car in this period. It is also interesting to contrast truck output patterns with those for autos. The domestic truck sector suffered an import related decline in the late 1970s which was similar in size and scope to that experienced in the auto market. Tariffs on imported trucks were raised from 4% to 25% in 1980 (Chapter II), through an administrative measure and by 1985 domestic truck output had returned to nearly its 1978 level. Although the truck makers clearly benefitted from new products (i.e., minivans) and shifting demand patterns in this period, it appears that the tariff on trucks may have provided more effective protection than did the voluntary restraints on auto imports.

16. This study assumes that reductions in output would reduce domestic job opportunities at the average rate of employment per unit assembled in the industry because of the large impacts identified here in both the intermediate and small car markets.

17. These indirect job losses result directly from input relationships with the auto industry and do not include Keynesian or income multiplier effects of the type found in macroeconomic models. Clearly, trade related job losses have significant ripple effects on the economy, as reflected in the general decline of older manufacturing regions of the U.S. during the period of high dollar values in the 1980-85 period.

CHAPTER VII
PUBLIC POLICY FOR THE AUTO INDUSTRY

This Chapter begins with a comparison of the final price and output effects of the VRAs across firms and size classes and then derives some general conclusions about the effects of the trade restraints and fuel economy regulations on the domestic auto industry during the period covered by this study. Transplant production in the U.S. and the long-run implications of expected rapid growth in transplant output will then be analyzed. The effects of market structure and non-competitive behavior on the competitiveness of the domestic industry and the possible impacts of alternative trade policies on these problems will then be considered. The Chapter ends with a summary of the lessons learned in this study.

The final simulations (Stage 3) of the direct and indirect effects of the VRAs and fuel economy regulations on price and output, by firm and size class, are summarized in Table 1. Chapter V argued that if the VRAs increased residual demand for any size-class of cars, for any domestic firm, then that firm faced a choice in how to respond. It could raise prices, raise output or both.[1] Table 1 provides an estimate of actual firm and industry performance under the VRAs.

One of the most surprising results of this study is that the effect of the VRAS on output was larger than their effect on prices in most cases, as shown in Table 1. This was true despite the fact that the regression coefficients for the direct effects of the VRAs were generally larger and more significant in the price equations than in the quantity equations. Thus it appears that the VRAs did stimulate domestic output and helped staunch the flow of job opportunities out of the domestic industry, if the effects in the large-car market are ignored for the reasons discussed in Chapter VI.

The exceptions to the general tendency for output effects to exceed price effects were all GM cases. In the short-run for small-cars, and both the short- and the long-run for intermediate models, GM prices increased by more than output under the VRAs. GM was also the only firm to sustain a substantial price increase in a case where the VRAs and fuel economy regulations caused output to fall. GM displayed a

TABLE 1
THE EFFECTS OF THE VRAS ON PRICE AND OUTPUT:
FINAL SIMULATIONS

	Quantity		Price	
	Short-run	Long-run	Short-run	Long-run
Small-GM	-0.8%	13.3%	10.6%	8.7%
Small-Ford	43.7%	33.4%	21.4%	18.7%
Small-Chrysler	68.8%	44.5%	13.8%	13.7%
Small-AM	144.5%	22.3%	1.8%	-1.6%
Medium-GM	4.8%	0.7%	14.0%	11.3%
Medium-Ford	-47.7%	-43.6%	-19.3%	-12.2%
Medium-Chrys.	-10.3%	28.3%	-1.8%	5.6%
Medium-AM	521.1%	1576.4%	-14.3%	-3.1%
Large-GM	-30.9%	-42.7%	4.1%	0.6%
Large-Ford	11.9%	18.6%	5.9%	13.4%
Large-Chyrs.	31.7%	-64.7%	0.6%	-1.5%
Total-GM	-10.6%	-14.3%	4.3%	-2.3%
Total-Ford	-2.3%	-5.8%	-5.5%	-1.6%
Total-Chrys.	31.3%	30.8%	1.7%	7.5%
Total-AM	192.1%	41.1%	2.5%	4.5%
Total-Domestic	-4.5%	-6.7%	0.7%	-2.0%
Total-Import	6.3%	-10.4%	7.4%	6.1%

stronger tendency to increase prices (rather than output) than the other firms in this study.

The results in Table 1 also show that the largest price effects of the VRAs occurred in the small-car market where there was direct competition with Japanese imports. The price effects were smaller in the intermediate market and smallest in the market for full-size and luxury cars, where there had been much less competition with Japanese imports.

These results contradict the common view that the VRAs had their biggest effect on the prices of large cars. The USITC (1985a) points out that the average prices of full-sized cars grew much more rapidly than other car prices during the VRAs. However, the results in Table 1 suggest that the VRAs had less effect on the *long-run trend rate of growth in real auto prices* in the large-car market than they did in the small-car market. The trend rate of growth may well have been higher for large car prices but that trend reflects factors other than the VRAs, such as pollution control costs (possibly higher on cars with large engines, since the same numerical emissions standards apply to all cars), the CAFE standards, gas guzzler tax and long-term growth in the income levels of the wealthier groups in the U.S. (yielding increased large-car demand, reduced price sensitivity and higher markups).[2]

Higher prices in the small car market were also the greatest weakness of the VRAs, in the long-run, because they undermined the ability of domestic producers to compete. Increased prices enhanced opportunities for future penetration of the domestic market by foreign producers. This opening is reflected in the dramatic increase in the number of Japanese owned auto-assembly plants operating in North America which were planned for the late 1980s and the early 1990s. Higher prices for domestic small cars also created an opportunity for producers in other countries (e.g. Korea and Brazil) to begin exporting cars to the U.S. and have also encouraged U.S. assemblers to invest in foreign assembly facilities designed to produce cars for the U.S. market, such as the Ford Plant in Mexico which assembles the Mercury Tracer station wagon for the U.S. market.[3]

The fact that small car prices were increased by the VRAs suggests that the industry did not eliminate the MCD during this period of protection. This is one of the most significant failures of the VRAs. Without improvements in efficiency and reductions in production costs the VRAs only served to delay the eventual loss of a greater share of the small car market to foreign-based producers. The only significant way in which the potential for ultimate foreign domination of the small car market was changed in the long-run by the VRAs was that it encouraged Japanese and other producers to build a substantial number of cars in the U.S. The dimensions of these building plans are indicative of the domestic industry's continuing competitive problems in the small car market.

A. The VRAs and Transplant Production in the U.S.

Japanese auto producers did not begin assembling cars and trucks in the U.S. until 1983, two years after the inception of the VRAs. Transplant production increased from 31,000 units in 1983 to 233,0000 units in 1986 and were increased dramatically in the 1988-1992 period. Some new job opportunities will be created as production in these facilities rises. Cost-effective production in these plants will also "vitiate the familiar arguments among managers and workers in existing facilities that success of foreign automakers is based on cultural and site-specific factors"[4] and will lead to increased experience with the Japanese system of organizing production.

In 1987 Japanese firms had plans to assemble 1,830,000 cars and trucks per year by 1990 in 7 U.S. plants (including two joint operations

(Ford/Mazda and Chrysler/Mitsubishi Motor). Four of these plants were in operation in 1987.[5] It is estimated that each of these plants will result in the direct and indirect employment of 6,700 workers (including parts supplying industries). Thus these plants will generate about 47,000 jobs by 1990 (about half in the auto industry and the rest in supplier firms). However, the UAW claims that the typical U.S. auto plant generates about 25,000 jobs, with the difference explained by the fact that most parts used in the Japanese assembly plants are imported. Thus the 7 plants will displace about 175,000 U.S. jobs, for a net loss of 128,000 jobs by 1990, if their output displaces production in domestic plants.

Five additional transplant assembly plants were planned or under construction in 1988 in Canada. These included one plant owned by a Korean-based firm (Hyundai), three plants owned by Japanese-based firms and a GM/Suzuki joint venture. The Canadian transplant facilities are designed to assemble an additional 660,000 units in 1990, with many of these destined for sale in the U.S, resulting in additional labor displacement beyond the 128,000 job opportunities at stake in U.S. transplants. Transplant production in North America exceeded 2,500,000 units in 1992. Approximately 3,200,000 cars were imported into the U.S. in the 1986 model year (out of total domestic car sales were about 10.9 million units). Import penetration of the U.S. market (including transplants) could rise from the 1986 level of 29% to almost half of the domestic market by the mid-1990s if the cars assembled in transplant facilities displace output from U.S.-based assemblers.[6]

B. Employment Prospects for the U.S. Auto Industry

Ultimate labor displacement in the 1985-2000 time-frame will depend on the ability of the domestic industry to respond to the competitive challenge of the Asian-based producers, and on the types of trade and other regulatory policies developed (or not developed) for this industry. The VRAs may have increased the potential Japanese and Korean shares of the U.S. auto market, in the long-run, because Japanese producers have gained experience in building compact and luxury cars under the VRAs and could potentially capture most of this market, and because Japanese firms and their Korean partners have the potential to dominate the subcompact market. In the compact and luxury segments perceived quality is probably as important (if not more so) than price competitiveness. Japanese producers have a better reputation for quality, than do U.S.-based firms. Ford, and to a lesser extent Chrysler, have made substantial progress in improving the quality of their products. GM's ability to achieve higher quality levels will be a critical determinant of whether or not the domestic-based industry as a whole is able to meet the import challenge in the small car market.

The parts purchasing behavior of foreign-owned assembly plants in the U.S. is another important determinant of future domestic employment opportunities. If the fall in the value of the dollar and new trade policies (such as local-content regulations) encourage the Japanese to buy a larger share of their parts and supplies in the U.S., then some of the job opportunities placed at risk by foreign direct investment can be retained in the U.S.

The final issue affecting the employment content of trade in the 1990s is the future of subcompact production in the U.S. Two questions will determine the outcome. First, can great strides be made in raising productivity levels in domestic production, through new technology programs such as the GM Saturn project? Second, will exchange rate policies be used to reduce the growing U.S. trade deficit with the Asian NICs, raising effective wages in these countries by devaluing the dollar against their currencies? These currencies moved with the dollar as it fell in the 1985-87 period, so there was no change in their comparative production costs.

Ultimately, Asian-based producers could capture at least 45% to 50% of the U.S. auto market in the 1990s. If market demand stays in the range of 10 million units per year, as in 1984, an additional 2 to 2.5 million units of domestic production could be displaced by transplants and imports in the 1990s. This increase in imports and transplant sales could displace 260,000 to 310,000 additional work-years of direct employment demand (at 1984 employment/output levels). The actual market shares of the Asian-based producers, and hence future domestic employment levels, will be determined by the industry's ability to close the cost and quality gaps in the 1985-2000 period, which will in turn be influenced by future trade and regulatory policies. This study has shown that the VRAs have not improved the long-run competitiveness of U.S.-based assemblers, and may have damaged it in several important ways. These results suggest that new trade, industrial and regulatory policies may be required to restore the competitiveness of this sector and preserve domestic job opportunities.

C. The Impacts of Alternative Policies

The discussion to this point has focused on the VRAs and one policy alternative, the option of no action. The simulation models presented in Chapter VI showed that both prices and output would generally have been lower for small and intermediate cars if the VRAs and fuel economy regulations had not been in effect.

One of the motivations for this study was a report that at the time the VRAs were being negotiated an executive with one of the "big-three" auto assembly firms approached the U.S. government to suggest that a tri-partite agreement be worked out with the major auto producers, the UAW and the government. This agreement would have included limitations on price and wage hikes as a quid pro quo in exchange for trade protection for the domestic industry.[7] This proposed agreement forms the basis for an alternative policy scenario in which wages and prices are fixed, in real terms.[8]

Simulations of a scenario with fixed wages and prices would require adjustments to the model which are beyond the scope of this study. However, some general observations can be made about the likely outcomes of such a scenario, based on intuition gained from working with the present model. Prices would be lower than the base case presented above (no quotas), by very substantial amounts, because of the high overall trend rate of growth in auto prices in the 1980s. Real wages would be only slightly lower than the base case because there was less growth in wages than in prices during this period. Output levels in the small and intermediate markets would have been higher than in either the base or VRA cases, because of the effects of lower prices. It is not clear that domestic producers could have earned sufficient profits to induce them to actually meet the higher levels of demand which would be achieved through price restraint. However, given the highly concentrated structure of the domestic industry and the markups that were being achieved under the VRAs, it seems reasonable to argue that domestic vehicle output could have been expanded to the level of output in 1978 (see Table 10, in Chapter VI above), which was 1.5 million units above actual 1985 output levels.

One additional policy measure which could have been added to the tripartite agreement to make it more attractive to the domestic auto industry would have been elimination of the Gas Guzzler Tax and possible relaxation of the CAFE standards, which were probably responsible for the decline in large car output under the VRAs. Crandall, Gruenspecht, Keeler and Lave (1986) argue that the fuel economy regulations were an inefficient mechanism for forcing technological innovation (to increase fuel economy) on the domestic auto industry, and that these standards were probably made more difficult to achieve by simultaneous tightening in auto emissions standards. The fuel economy regulations put a much greater burden on domestic producers--especially GM--with their larger average car sizes, than on the manufacturers of the smaller imported models. A gasoline tax would have been a more efficient mechanism for encouraging energy conservation, and might have allowed the domestic auto industry to devote increased resources to improving quality and efficiency to meet the challenges of foreign competition and the MCD.

The Gas Guzzler Tax creates clear-cut incentives for reduced sales of domestic large cars, thus penalizing domestic producers to the extent that consumers in the market for large cars switch to imported luxury models. The effects of the CAFE standards on total domestic production are more ambiguous than those of the Gas Guzzler Tax. Some analysts have referred to the CAFE standards as a form of domestic content legislation for U.S.-based firms, because these regulations are applied separately to imported and domestically produced product lines of each manufacturer. In theory, the CAFE standards create incentives for U.S.-based firms to expand domestic production of small cars in order to raise the average fuel economy of the cars they sell in the U.S. This feature discourages U.S.-based firms from engaging in substantial sales of "captive import" small cars. The CAFE standards also clearly create incentives for firms to downsize and increase the fuel efficiency of their entire product lines, and to move large car production "offshore" (e.g. to Canada).

This study has shown that the sales of large most cars, and of Ford intermediates, fell dramatically during the period of the VRAs. These negative effects are large enough to outweigh any positive effects of the VRAs on small and intermediate car production in the U.S. Thus fuel economy regulations seem to be associated with a major reduction in overall auto output in the U.S. This is an unexpected consequence, particularly for the CAFE standards, and should give policy makers reason to re-evaluate all regulatory approaches to reducing domestic gasoline consumption. These findings confirm and strengthen the conclusions of Crandall, *et al* (1986) regarding the effectiveness of direct fuel economy regulations.

It is also important to note that if the CAFE standards were to be eliminated a major surge could be anticipated in captive auto imports by the Big Three U.S. assemblers. If sudden dislocations in the patterns of domestic auto production are to be avoided then it will be necessary to relax the CAFE standards *only* as part of a more comprehensive package of policies designed to help restructure the domestic auto industry.

Some observers of the domestic industry have suggested that the VRAs were fundamentally flawed because the domestic industry's basic problem stemmed from a shortage of competition and that the VRAs *reduced* competitive forces in the domestic auto market. The simulations in this Chapter show that eliminating the VRAs would have resulted in lower prices, but domestic output would also have been reduced. The issue which must then be addressed is: 'Would no protection have been the most effective mechanism for promoting competition in the domestic auto industry?'. The results of this study provide some insights into this issue and suggest some additional policy options that should be considered if the domestic industry requests relief when transplant production increases in the 1990s in the U.S.

D. Market Structure and Efficiency

The three size classes of cars considered in this study appear to represent distinct products, from an economic point of view. The degree of interdependence of pricing, sensitivity to changes in import prices and macroeconomic factors and response to changes in factor costs are all quite different in each of these markets, as shown in Chapter V. While there are clearly substitution effects between these classes, these effects are much smaller than the substitution effects within a size-class. The nature of competition and the way in which it was affected by the VRAs and fuel economy regulations must be considered separately for each of these three markets.

This study has shown that under the VRAs there were several indications of oligopoly behavior and associated welfare losses. The implied estimates of demand elasticities for small car output, discussed in Chapter V, suggest that under the VRAs the structure of the small car markets gave substantial market power to both GM and Ford, despite foreign competition. These are only inferred results, and require confirmation with traditional demand studies, but the inference was strong and consistent with observed market shares.

Performance in all three markets also suggests that domestic producers had substantial market power after the VRAs were implemented, because the VRAs caused price increases in most cases. If these markets were competitively structured then we would expect to see the quota's having a much larger effect on output than on price, especially in the long-run. Yet the long-run the effects of the VRAs on the output of domestic producers (excepting transplant production) were smaller than the short-run effects.

Examination of pricing trends and analysis of regression results both suggest some evidence of price-leadership behavior in the domestic industry. GM was the apparent price leader and was also more predisposed to raising prices under the VRAs than the other domestic producers. The simulation results generated several cases where GM, alone, had a greater rate of price than output growth under the VRAs. The VRAs had a greater effect on output than on prices in all cases for the other domestic producers.

Import competition has been largely restricted to the small and luxury car markets in the past and this will continue to be the case in the future. The results of this study suggest that the VRAs had a positive effect on prices and output for all domestic producers except Ford intermediate cars, suggesting that VRA-related quality upgrading was largely confined to the subcomponents of the small car market (with imports upgrading from the subcompact to the compact and luxury sports car markets). Small cars, while important, represented less than half of the total number of units sold by domestic producers during the period of the VRAs, as shown in Table 2. If the VRAs had not been implemented competition would have increased substantially in the small car market as import penetration increased. Yet the potential for non-competitive outcomes in this market would have persisted even in the absence of trade protection because of brand loyalties, regional differences in demand patterns and limited numbers of substitutes for some small cars (for example sports models such as the Camaro and the Mustang). In the long-run the VRAs will cause a *substantial increase* competition in the small car market because of the growth of transplant production in North America.

Thus the principal effect of the VRAs on market structure was to postpone increased competition in the small car markets. Competition will increase substantially in the future, at a cost of probable reductions in the number of domestic job opportunities.

TABLE 2
AVERAGE SALES SHARES BY SIZE CLASS,
1980:IV TO 1986:III

Size Class:	Share of Domestic Makes	Total U. S. Sales
Small Cars	45.6%	60.1%
Intermediates	31.4%	23.0%
Large Cars	23.1%	16.9%

Overall, the VRAs had little impact on problems of concentration in the intermediate and large car markets. Without the VRAs U.S. producers would have become increasingly isolated in the large and intermediate markets and would have ceded much of the market for smaller cars to foreign-based auto assemblers in the 1980s (including those making captive imports). This effect was postponed under the VRAs, but it is still likely to occur in the 1990s. The principal difference is that a much larger share of the small cars sold in the U.S. by foreign Multinationals will be assembled in North America. Without the VRAs most of these cars would have been imported directly from Japan, and the import share would have risen faster in the 1980s than it did under trade protection.

The U.S. auto industry has been one of the most concentrated sectors of the domestic economy in the post World War II era. This concentration has resulted in higher domestic prices and reduced ability to innovate and respond to international competitive pressures. Despite the tremendous growth in imports during the 1970s it appears that market concentration would have remained a problem in the intermediate and large car markets in the 1990s whether or not the VRAs were implemented. The most fundamental flaw of the VRAs, as an industrial policy, was their failure to do anything about the problems of concentration in this industry and its effects on the competitiveness of U.S.-based producers in the international automobile industry. The costs of concentration have been well documented in a number of excellent studies of the organization of this industry. White (1971) concluded in his seminal study that:

> "Fundamentally, this concentrated oligopoly is going to continue to behave and perform much as it has in the past, as long as it remains concentrated. Consequently, if we want improved performance, we must look to measures that will loosen the oligopoly and increase the number of independent centers of initiative in the industry. This can be achieved by lowering the barriers to entry or by creating more independent firms from among those already in existence. Both types of action would require structural remedies. The presumption here is that more centers of initiative would increase the likelihood of meaningful price competition, leading to lower prices, lower profits, and a better allocation of resources; more centers would also increase the likelihood of faster technological progress and faster response to changes in consumer tastes."

While there have been vast changes in the structure of the small car markets because of increased imports in the 17 years since White's study, the markets for intermediate and large cars remain essentially unchanged, in terms of oligopoly structure and performance. The VRAs had little impact on the oligopoly problem in the U.S. intermediate and large car markets and White's conclusions remain appropriate prescriptions for these markets in 1990s.

There may be an opportunity to implement structural remedies in the auto industry in the near future without having to resort to government suit to break up one or more auto companies. Transplant production capacity in North America is projected to increase to more than 2,500,000 units a year by the early 1990s, as discussed above. Most of the transplants will be producing cars for the U.S. market, which will dramatically increase competition in this market segment. There will be tremendous overcapacity in the domestic small car market but it is unlikely that this surplus will have significant effects on the large and intermediate car sectors, the most concentrated markets, which seem to display the worst conduct problems.

Transplant facilities create a much smaller number of direct and indirect job opportunities than does a typical U.S. assembly plant, in part because most of the major components used in these plants are usually imported from the home country of the plant's owner. As a result of the threat of labor displacement the UAW has already increased its lobbying and education efforts in support of domestic content legislation.

One or more of the U.S.-based assemblers is likely to join the UAW in its calls for more protection of the domestic market as the dislocations rise in the domestic auto industry in the 1990s. An agreement requiring divestiture by one or more of the U.S.-based assemblers could be required by the government as a *quid pro quo* for more protection for the domestic industry. GM, in particular, is a logical candidate for divestiture, and could be broken up into two or more assemblers with complete vertically integrated product lines (i.e. Chevrolet/NUMMI/Oldsmobile/Cadillac and GEO/Buick/Pontiac/Saturn). The essential element of this type of divestiture would be measures designed to increase competition in the those segments of the domestic industry which do not presently face significant foreign competition.

The precedent for this type of successful break-up was established in the AT&T divestiture agreements. Although those agreements were the result of a long-standing court suit, other pressures could be brought to bear to encourage GM to participate in such an agreement. Not the least of these might be stockholder pressure. GM has suffered a continual erosion in its market share during the VRAs from an average of 45.8% of the total domestic auto market in the 1981 model year to 41.7% in 1986, and it has continued to decline to 34.8% in 1987 and 34.4% in 1988.[9] In contrast, Ford's market share increased by 1.1 percentage points to 18% in 1986, 19.7% in 1978 and 20.8% in 1988, while Chrysler's share was enlarged by 1.8 points to 10.5% in 1986, and then level off in 1987 and 1988.[10] As a result, GM informed the UAW in 1986 that it may close up to nine U.S. assembly plants in the next few years.[11]

GM may simply be too large to innovate efficiently, and it appears to be biased in favor of expensive investments in new production technology (i.e. robotics and computer integrated manufacturing) and unwilling to undertake fundamental changes in its management structure and labor relations. As a result, labor productivity in its new plants is apparently lower than productivity in less capital intensive plants built by other U.S. producers in recent years. According to work in progress by the MIT auto project there is a wide disparity in the average efficiency of new auto plants built in the U.S. in recent years.[12] One firm (presumably GM, although this could not be revealed in the study) tended to have more capital intensive plants than other firms, but these plants were not the most efficient in terms of labor productivity among the new plants. The decline in GM's market share and its relative inefficiency vis-a-vis domestic rivals may be the result of its operating for too long in a protected domestic environment where rapid innovation was not necessary for its survival.

GM's stockholders could gain from divestiture if the losses of its oligopoly rents (through lower prices) were offset by increases in the efficiency and overall market share of the prospective "GM-daughters". GM may be the firm with the most to loose, in terms of market share and potential sales, with the increase in transplant production in the U.S. in the 1990s.

Divestiture is unlikely to come about as a result of market forces (i.e. through a leveraged buyout). A private GM buyout would dwarf such mammoth transactions as the $25 billion KKR buyout of RJ-Reynolds/Nabisco in total size. More importantly, it may be too late for a private buyout to rescue GM from its competitive decline. Transplant production was already increasing dramatically in 1987 and 1988, and was responsible for a large portion of GM's decline in this period. The growth in transplants will accelerate in the 1988-1992 period, and GM's production plans and product offerings for this period are already set. Thus a GM divestiture would only be feasible as part of a comprehensive public policy package designed to address the fundamental competitive problems of the domestic auto industry. It would require some form of limited government protection of the domestic market (ie further quotas, tariffs and/or domestic content agreements) to work. In the absence of such an agreement, GM's market share will probably continue to decline in the 1990s, and with it the total level of output and employment in the U.S. auto industry.

E. Summary

The VRAs increased both the price and output levels of domestic producers in the small and intermediate segments of the U.S. auto market. The output effects estimated here are somewhat larger than those estimated in other studies of the VRAs, and generally exceeded the price effects for most producers. Domestic output of large cars was apparently reduced during the VRAs. This decline was probably the result of a number of factors besides the VRAs, including the CAFE Standards, Gas Guzzler Tax, lagged changes in demand patterns resulting from higher oil prices, and the tendency of domestic producers to raise prices in spite of declining output.

A significant number of job opportunities were preserved in the domestic auto industry by the VRAs during the 1981-1986 period. The estimates generated here of the direct employment effects of the VRAs are slightly larger than those of in some of the previous studies of this issue. However, all other studies overlook the indirect employment effects of increased domestic production on employment in supplier industries. When these effects are properly accounted for the VRAs are seen to have saved perhaps three to six times as many jobs during the period of the quotas as estimated in previous research on this topic. The large actual and potential effects of trade on employment in this industry helps to explain the broad political support for the VRAs, despite widespread objections from the economics profession to all forms of trade protection. These employment impacts are also a major reasons why further efforts to improve the competitiveness of the domestic industry are both likely to develop in the future and socially desirable.

Both social welfare and industrial competitiveness could be improved by measures which decrease concentration in the domestic auto industry. The competitive problems of the U.S. auto industry can be traced, in part, to the domination of the U.S. auto market by three domestic firms during the post-war era. The industry's oligopoly structure has resulted in higher prices for consumers, and it has reduced the incentives for firms to innovate and reduce costs. The contrast with Japan's auto industry, with nine domestic producers initially serving an economy that was less than half the size of the U.S. auto market, helps to explain the competitive difficulties of U.S.-based assemblers in the 1990s.

The VRAs have had little long-run impact on the competitive structure of the domestic auto market. In the late 1970s it became clear that domestic producers could no longer compete in large segments of the small car market. The VRAs postponed the ultimate foreign capture of the U.S. small car market until sometime in the 1990s, and probably worsened the competitive problems of the domestic industry by expanding the range of products for which there was foreign competition and by creating conditions which favored the growth of export-based auto producers in several NIC-locations. However, the VRAs had little long-run impact on the intermediate and large car markets, which represented over half of domestic output in 1986.

The competitive problems of the domestic industry were clearly symbolized by the Manufacturing Cost Differential between U.S. and Japanese small car producers which was discussed in Chapter II. The MCD reflected both labor cost problems and a productivity gap between U.S. and Japanese producers. The VRAs did not have any significant effect on UAW labor costs, although total labor costs fell slightly at Ford and Chrysler and rose slightly at GM because of changes in white collar compensation and labor force composition. Thus the VRAs did not have a significant, direct effect on the labor cost gap. This study did not directly address the productivity gap. However, the fact that the VRAs increased the average prices of most domestic small cars suggests that output per worker did not increase rapidly during this period.

The VRAs did increase the capital cost, and probably the profitability, of both Ford and Chrysler.[13] However, it is likely that higher profits are a short-run phenomena resulting from the temporary protection of the small car market and from the particular difficulties GM has faced in complying with fuel economy regulations in the mid-1980s. As transplant production grows dramatically in the next five years these abnormal profits are likely to disappear. These facts are clearly perceived in the U.S. financial markets, where the domestic auto producers have some of the lowest price/earning ratios of firms in any U.S. manufacturing industry, despite the recent record profits and the high degree of concentration in this sector.

As transplant production in the U.S. increases in the next five years labor displacement is likely to increase. Industry employment is likely to resume its long-run decline, relative to peak levels achieved in 1978, after achieving a brief plateau in the mid-1980s under the VRAs. Domestic auto producers may fare better than their employees in the 1990s, if they are able to shed excess capacity and concentrate their efforts in the unique North American intermediate and large car markets where they still maintain a comparative advantage. Consumers will continue to pay high prices for these products as a result of the oligopoly structure in this market.

As labor displacement rises in the U.S. auto assembly industry, and in related parts and materials supply sectors, pressures for increased trade protection will increase. Local content measures are likely to receive the greatest attention in the political arena because of the direct connections between transplant production and employment declines. Consumers in the U.S. and displaced workers in the affected industries would be better served by a broader set of policies designed to address the fundamental market structure problems and related competitive difficulties of the U.S. auto industry.

The U.S. government passed up an opportunity to obtain *quid pro quos* from domestic producers and workers in exchange for the VRAs. An important opportunity to increase domestic competitiveness was therefore missed. The U.S. government has had a passive industrial policy for the auto industry for four decades in its failure to challenge the highly unusual levels of concentration in this industry. It is thus partially responsible for the industry's present competitive difficulties. Perhaps the next opportunity will not be overlooked when the auto industry and its workers return to Washington to request further protection from transplant and import problems in the 1990s.

NOTES

1. It is possible that output would fall and prices rise, if market power were increased by the VRAs (i.e., if the slope of the residual demand curve increased significantly). Prices could also be reduced and output increased if the residual demand curve facing a firm were to become flatter.

2. The time trends in the price equations estimated in Chapter V were generally small and insignificant. Most of the long-run shifts in prices were reflected in the coefficients for real gnp (LOGGNP8). The GNP coefficients increased from the small through intermediate to the large size class for each of the big-three firms (except for large Chryslers). Thus, as real income grew over time, the prices of most large cars tended to grow faster than those of small cars.

3. *Wards Communications, Inc.*, (1988), p.211.

4. Alan Altshuler, *et al,* (1984).

5. The transplant data in this section are from the UAW Research Department (1987).

6. Note that total auto sales in 1986 were a cyclical peak, and that transplant production capacity will exceed 2,500,000 in North America by the mid-1990s, so the estimate of a 50% potential market share for foreign-based firms is a conservative ceiling.

7. This proposal was reported in private interviews with John Zysman and Laura Tyson, principal investigators with the Berkeley Roundtable on International Economy. The proposal was rejected by representatives of the Reagan Administration.

8. The alternative scenario would have to incorporate some mechanism for adjusting real prices over time to reflect changes in the costs of complying with emissions control, safety and fuel economy regulations. This is a major practical problem because there is a substantial debate about the actual costs of, and appropriate pricing for, these regulation-induced design changes. This problem serves to underscore the importance of providing for improved access to detailed, firm level accounting data as part of any such agreement.

9. *Automotive News,* January 9, 1989, p.4.

10. *ibid.*

11. *The Wall Street Journal,* November 11, 1986.

12. John E. Krafcik, "Manufacturing Automobiles: State of the Art Technology, U.S. Technology and the Prospects for Convergence", remarks to the Maryland Seminar on the American Economy, October 4, 1988.

13. GM's capital costs were reduced slightly by the VRAs and its market share declined during this period.

BIBLIOGRAPHY

Abernathy, W.J., J.E. Harbour, and I.M. Henn. 1981. "Productivity and Comparative Cost Advantages: Some Estimates for Major Automotive Producers," Harvard Business School Working Paper.

Aizcorbe, Ana, Clifford Winston and Ann Friedlaender. 1987. "Cost Competitiveness of the U.S. Automobile Industry," in *Blind Intersection? Policy and the Automobile Industry,* by Clifford Winston and Associates. Washington, D.C.: The Brookings Institution.

Altshuler, Alan, Martin Anderson, Daniel Jones, Daniel Roos, and James Womack. 1984. *The Future of the Automobile: The Report of MIT's International Automobile Program.* Cambridge, Mass.: MIT Press.

Appelbaum, E. 1979. "Testing Price Taking Behavior," *Journal of Econometrics* 9: 283-294.

Appelbaum, E. 1982. "The Estimation of the Degree of Oligopoly Power," *Journal of Econometrics* 19: 287-299.

Automotive News. Various years. "Market Databook Issue," April.

Baker, Jonathan B. and Timothy F. Bresnahan. 1985a. "The Gains from Merger or Collusion in Product-Differentiated Industries", *The Journal of Industrial Economics* 23, no. 4 (June): 427-444.

Baker, Jonathan B. and Timothy F. Bresnahan. 1985b. "Estimating the Elasticity of Demand Facing a Single Firm." Palo Alto, Cal.: Dept. of Economics, Stanford University, October.

Beach, Charles M. and James G. MacKinnon. 1978. "A Maximum Likelihood Procedure for Regression with Autocorrelated Errors," *Econometrica* 46: 51-58.

Board of Governors of the Federal Reserve System. Various years. *Foreign Exchange Rates, G.5(405).*

Branson, William, and James Love. 1986. "Dollar Appreciation and Manufacturing Employment and Output," National Bureau of Economic Research Working Paper No. 1972, Cambridge, Mass., July.

Bresnahan, T. F. 1981a. "Competition and Collusion in the American Automobile Market: The 1955 Price War" Research Paper No. 2, Stanford Workshop on the Economics of Factor Markets, Department of Economics, Stanford University, Palo Alto, Cal., February.

Bresnahan, T.F. 1981b. "Identification of Market Power," Research Paper No. 15, Stanford Workshop on Factor Markets, Stanford University, Palo Alto, Cal., October.

Citibase: Citibank Economic Databank. 1978. New York: Citicorp Data Base Services. Machine-readable data file.

Cole, Robert E., and Taizo Yakushiji. 1984. *The American and Japanese Industries in Transition: Report of the Joint U.S.-Japan Automotive Study.* Ann Arbor, Mich.: Center for Japanese Studies, University of Michigan.

Council of Economic Advisors. 1986. *Economic Report of the President.* Washington, D.C.: U.S. Government Printing Office, February.

Crandall, Robert W., 1984. "Import Quotas and the Automobile Industry: The Costs of Protectionism." *The Brookings Review* (Summer): 8-16.

_____. 1986. "Detroit Rode Quotas to Prosperity" *The Wall Street Journal* (January 29).

_____, Howard K. Gruenspect, Theodore E. Keeler and Lester B. Lave. 1986. *Regulating the Automobile.* Washington, D.C.: The Brookings Institution.

Dornbusch, Rudiger and Stanley Fischer. 1987 *Macroeconomics.* New York: McGraw Hill Book Company.

Dickens, William T. 1988. "The Effects of Trade on Employment: Techniques and Evidence," in *The Dynamics of Trade and Employment,* ed. Laura D'Andrea Tyson, William T. Dickens and John Zysman. Cambridge, Mass.: Ballinger Publishing Company.

Edmund's New Car Prices. Various years. West Hempstead, New York.

Feenstra, Robert C. 1984. "Voluntary Export Restraint in U.S. Autos, 1980-81: Quality, Employment and Welfare Effects", in *The Structure and Evolution of Recent U.S. Trade Policy,* ed. Robert E. Baldwin and Anne O. Krueger. Cambridge, MA: National Bureau of Economic Research.

_____. 1985a. "Automobile Prices and Protection: The U.S.-Japan Trade Restraint." *Journal of Policy Modeling* 7, no. 1: 49-68.

_____. 1985b. "Quality Change under Trade Restraints: Theory and Evidence from Japanese Autos." Discussion Paper #298, Department of Economics. Columbia University, New York, August.

Flynn, Michael S. 1982. "Differentials in Vehicles' Landed Costs: Japanese Vehicles in the U.S. Marketplace." Working Paper Series No. 3, Center for Japanese Studies, University of Michigan, October 30.

Freeman, R. Edward and Daniel R. Gilbert, Jr. 1987. "Managing Stakeholder Relationships," in *Business and Society: Dimensions of Conflict and Cooperation,* ed. S. Prakash Sethi and Cecilia M. Falbe. Lexington, Mass.: Lexington Books.

Friedman, James W. 1977. *Oligopoly and the Theory of Games.* New York: North-Holland Publishing Company.

Fuss, Melvyn and Leonard Waverman. 1982. "The Extent and Sources of Cost and Efficiency Differences Between U.S. and Japanese Automobile Producers", National Bureau of Economic Research Working Paper No. 1849, Cambridge, Mass., December.

Gelfand, M.D. and P.T. Spiller. 1985. "Entry Barriers and Oligopolistic Strategies," Draft Working Paper, Hoover Institution, Palo Alto, Cal., July.

Gollop, F. and M. Roberts. 1979. "Firm Interdependence in Oligopolistic Markets," *Journal of Econometrics* 10: 313-331.

Gomez-Ibanez, Jose A., Robert A. Leone and Stephen A. O'Connell. 1983. "Restraining Auto Imports: Does Anyone Win?", *Journal of Policy Analysis and Management* 2, no. 2: 196-219.

Grossman, Gene M. 1982. "The Employment and Wage Effects of Import Competition in the United States." National Bureau of Economic Research Working Paper No. 1041, Cambridge, Mass., December.

Henderson, David R. 1985. "The Economics of Fuel Economy Standards." *Regulation* 9, no. 1 (January/February): 45-48.

Howes, Candace. 1993. *Japanese Auto Transplants and the U.S. Automobile Industry.* Washington, D.C.: The Economic Policy Institute, forthcoming.

Hwang, H. 1984. "Intra-industry Trade and Oligopoly: A Conjectural Variations Approach," *Canadian Journal of Economics* 17 (February): 126-137.

Iwata, G. 1984. "Measurement of Conjectural Variations in Oligopoly," *Econometrica* 42: 947-966.

Just, R. and W. Chern. 1980. "Tomatoes, Technology and Oligopoly," *The Bell Journal of Economics* 11: 584-602.

Kelley Blue Book New Car Price Manual. Various years. Irvine, CA.

Kreinin, Mordechai E. 1984. "Wage Competitiveness in the U.S. Auto and Steel Industries." *Contemporary Policy Issues* No. 4 (January): 39-50.

Kwoka, John L., Jr. 1984. "Market Power and Market Change in the U.S. Automobile Industry." *Journal of Industrial Economics* 32, no. 4 (June): 509-22.

Lawrence, Robert Z. 1984. *Can America Compete?* Washington, D.C.: Brookings Institution.

Mannering, Fred and Clifford Winston, 1987. "Economic Effects of Voluntary Export Restrictions," in *Blind Intersection? Policy and the Automobile Industry,* by Clifford Winston and Associates. Washington, D.C.: The Brookings Institution.

Martin, J.P., and J. Evans. 1981. "Notes on Measuring the Employment Displacement Effects of Trade by the Accounting Procedure." *Oxford Economic* Papers 33, no. 1: 154-64.

McGhee, John S. 1988 *Industrial Organization.* Englewood Cliffs, New Jersey: Prentice-Hall.

New York Times, 1986. February 13.

Pindyck, Robert S. and Daniel L. Rubinfeld. 1981. *Econometric Models and Economic Forecasts.* New York: McGraw-Hill Book Company.

Prestowitz, Jr., Clyde, and Paul Willen. 1992. *The Future of the U.S. Auto Industry: It Can Compete, Can It Survive?* Washington D.C.: The Economic Strategy Institute, June.

"Rise in Car Exports Confirmed by Japan." 1985. *New York Times,* March 29.

Scott, Robert E. 1988. "Trade and Employment in Automobiles: The Short-Run Success and Long-Run Failure of Protectionist Measures", in *The Dynamics of Trade and Employment,* ed. Laura D'Andrea Tyson, William T. Dickens and John Zysman. Cambridge, Mass.: Ballinger Publishing Company.

_____. 1993. "The Effects of Protection on a Domestic Oligopoly: The Case of the U.S. Auto Market", forthcoming, *Journal of Policy Modeling*.

Spiller, P.T. and E. Favaro. 1984 "The Effects of Entry Regulation on Oligopolistic Interaction: The Uruguayan Banking Sector," *The Rand Journal of Economics* 15, no. 2 (Summer): 244-254.

Standard and Poor's Compustat Services, Inc. Various years. *Compustat Annual Tapes.*

Stokes, Bruce. "Protection for a Price." *National Journal*, April 4, 1992: 794-799.

"Strong Yen Spurs Parts Imports from NICs, China." 1986. *Japan Economic Journal*, October 11.

Sullivan, D. 1985. "Testing Hypotheses about Firm Behavior in the Cigarette Industry," *Journal of Political Economy* 93: 586-598.

Sumner, D.A. 1981. "Measurement of Monopoly Behavior: An Application to the Cigarette Industry," *Journal of Political Economy* 89, (October): 1010-1019.

Takacs, Wendy E., and Ellen P. Tanzer. 1986. "Structural Change in the Demand for Automobiles by Size Class." *Quarterly Review of Economics and Business* 26, no. 3 (Autumn): 48-57.

Tarr, David G., and Morris E. Morkre. 1984. *Aggregate Costs to the United States of Tariffs and Quotas on Imports: General Tariff Cuts and Removal of Quotas on Automobiles, Steel, Sugar, and Textiles.* Bureau of Economics Staff Report to the Federal Trade Commission. Washington, D.C.: FTC, December.

Toder, Eric J., with Nicholas Scott Cardell and Ellen Burton. 1978. *Trade Policy and the U.S. Automobile Industry.* New York: Praeger Publishers.

United Auto Workers Research Department. 1987. "U.S. Auto Jobs: The Problem is Bigger than Japanese Imports." January 12. Mimeo.

_____. 1988. "Private Communication." July.

U.S. Dept. of Commerce, Bureau of Economic Analysis. Various years. "National Income and Product Accounts of the U.S., 1929-84," in the *Survey of Current Business.*

_____. Various years. *News Release on Capacity Utilization.*

U.S. Dept. of Labor, Bureau of Labor Statistics. Various years. *Consumer Price Index.*

_____. 1985a. *Employment, Hours, and Earnings, 1909-1984,* Vol. 1, Bulletin 1312-12, March.

_____. 1985b. "B.L.S. Employment Requirements, Table (9EMPLOYE1984P)," Office of Economic Growth and Employment Projections, October 7. Mimeo.

_____. 1985c. *Employment and Wages: Annual Averages 1984,* Bulletin 2249, November.

_____. 1986. *Supplement to Employment and Earnings,* (June).

U.S. Department of Transportation. 1981. *The U.S. Automobile Industry, 1980.* Report to the President from the Secretary of Transportation. DOT P-10 81 02. Washington, D.C.: Department of Transportation, March.

_____. 1982. *The U.S. Automobile Industry, 1981.* Report to the President from the Secretary of Transportation. DOT-P-10 82 01. Washington, D.C.: Department of Transportation, May.

U.S. International Trade Commission. Various years. *The U.S. Automobile Industry: Monthly Report on Selected Economic Indicators* (Report to the Subcommittee on Trade, Committee on Ways and Means, under investigation number 332-207 under section 332 of the Tariff Act of 1930), USITC Publication 2063. Washington, D.C.: U.S. International Trade Commission.

_____. 1985a. *A Review of Recent Developments in the U.S. Automobile Industry Including an Assessment of the Japanese Voluntary Restraint Agreements.* USITC Publication 1648. Washington, D.C.: U.S. International Trade Commission, February.

_____. 1985b. *The Internationalization of the Automobile Industry and Its Effects on the U.S. Automobile Industry.* USITC Publication 1712. Washington, D.C.: U.S. International Trade Commission, June.

_____. 1985c. *The U.S. Automotive Industry: U.S. Factory Sales, Retail Sales, Imports, Exports, Apparent Retail Prices, and Trade Balances with Selected Countries for Motor Vehicles, 1964-84.* USITC Publication 1762. Washington, D.C.: U.S. International Trade Commission, October.

Ward's Automotive Reports. Various years.

Ward's Communications Inc. Various years. *Ward's Automotive Yearbook.*

White, Lawrence J. 1971. *The Automobile Industry since 1945.* Cambridge, Mass.: Harvard University Press.

Winston, Clifford. 1987. *Blind Intersection?: Policy and the Automobile Industry.* Washington, D.C.: Brookings Institution.

Womack, James P., Daniel T. Jones and Daniel Roos. 1991. *The Machine that Changed the World.* New York: Macmillan.

INDEX

167

For Product Safety Concerns and Information please contact our EU
representative GPSR@taylorandfrancis.com Taylor & Francis Verlag GmbH,
Kaufingerstraße 24, 80331 München, Germany

Printed and bound by CPI Group (UK) Ltd, Croydon, CR0 4YY
08/05/2025
01864380-0005